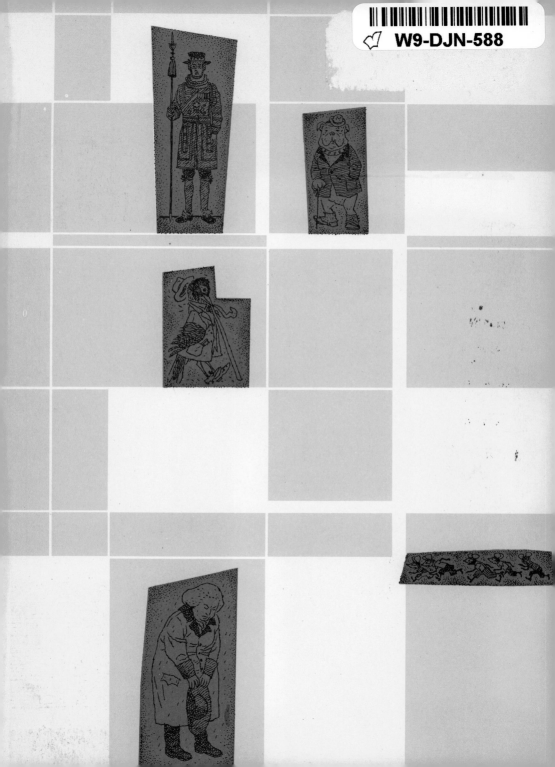

52
STORY
SERMONS

Benjamin P. Browne

52
STORY
SERMONS

Illustrations by
Oliver F. Grimley

THE JUDSON PRESS
PHILADELPHIA   CHICAGO   LOS ANGELES

This book is dedicated to Cynthia,
Mark, Wendy, Patsy, Bobby, Bunny,
Larry, Ricky, Vicky, and Debby,
ten grandchildren scattered
from Maine to California, whose
presence in this world, though
they are usually far away from
me, adds immensely to the joy
and delight of living.

ACKNOWLEDGMENTS

These junior stories come out of a pastoral ministry of over twenty-five years. Most of the stories I wrote and told to the children of my congregations. They are, therefore, stories that have been used and tested, and are here offered as aids to busy pastors and Sunday church school and vacation school teachers who are eagerly searching for junior stories.

In order to provide fifty-two stories, one for each Sunday of the year, ten stories have been adapted from JUNIORS, selected by Margie Ward. These stories, together with several others which have been adapted from suggestions of friends, are acknowledged at the end of the story. Since pastors and social workers today are frequently called upon to talk to boys in reform schools and penitentiaries, a modern interpretation of the Prodigal Son has been included as tested in a service for boys in the Philadelphia Youth Study Center.

My special thanks are due to the invaluable editorial service of my able assistant, Margaret Sherwood Ward, and to the encouragement and comments of Marion Brawn, Director of Children's Publications. Here also I am under debt to Dr. Miles W. Smith, Book Editor, for his counsel and craftsmanship.

I am grateful to Oliver Grimley, well-known artist, whose drawings enliven many of the stories, and to Miss Florence Pharo for her assistance in proofreading the galleys.

BENJAMIN P. BROWNE

CONTENTS

INTRODUCTION

STORY SERMONS

STORIES FOR ANY TIME

CHAPTER 1

the pastor and his church children

THE PASTOR WHO loves the children of his congregation has at least five ways in which he may minister to them and lead them into participation in the church service of worship.

Perhaps the method most widely used is: (1) the junior story sermon; but there are also (2) the pastor's prayer with the children, (3) the children's illustration in the adult sermon, (4) the hymn for the children, and (5) the children's choirs.

Resource materials for the first four of the above methods are generously provided in this book, together with suggestions for cooperation with the Sunday church school in order to make the use of these resources most effective and meaningful to the boys and girls of the congregation.

Fifty-two New Stories

For pastors who regularly give a brief story to the children of their congregation, this book provides a suitable story for each Sunday of the year—fifty-two stories. Tens of thousands of pastors are using this method and will, therefore, welcome a series of fresh stories which take only from three to five minutes for the telling and include a wide range of Christian truth.

These stories are also prepared for use by teachers in the Sunday church school, in the vacation church school, and in other forms of junior activities.

Pastoral Prayers for Children

Many pastors, however, instead of telling a junior story, prefer to pray with the children whom they gather around them at the front of the sanctuary, just before they dismiss them from morning worship to the Sunday church school extended session. Prayers in language within the child's experience are given in this book as suggestions to aid busy pastors. Some of the prayers are arranged for seasons and anniversaries. They are given a variety of expression to help avoid the trite and the stale. Children will better participate in the pastor's prayer for them, if the ideas and words are fresh rather than hackneyed. Children's minds grow listless under clichés. These prayers are not so much provided to be read as to offer hints and suggestions for prayer themes.

Sermon Illustrations

Still other pastors have preferred to use children's illustrations in their regular sermons rather than to employ either of the above methods. These pastors have taken cognizance of the objections of many educators in the children's field to the use of the junior story in morning worship. Some children's specialists feel that the story is injected into the service from the outside to entertain the children. They see it as something not an integral part of the worship.

Many such educators advocate, however, integrating the children into participation in worship by means of the pastor using, in his so-called "adult sermon," illustrations drawn from the experience of children and within the range of their interests and level of understanding. The idea is to make the children of the congregation aware that the sermon is for them, too, and if they listen, they will find it is addressed to them as part of the family worshiping God. Therefore, this book has a chapter giving resources of such illustrations.

Moreover, this chapter shows how many of the junior stories given here can also be used as vivid anecdotes or illustrations in the adult sermon. Nearly all of the stories in this book have been written to be adaptable to use in the adult sermon for pastors who prefer to use this method rather than the junior story by itself.

Hymn Stories

There are pastors who, in addition to using any one of the above methods, are also alert to the spiritual values of the congregational singing of hymns familiar to children—hymns in the singing of which the children enter with exultant gladness and an inspiring sense of offering worshipful praise to God. A group of stories in this book shows how the hymns can be adapted to the children's joyful participation in the church family worship, and how often stories can be built around them to make them meaningful in new ways to children. Suggestions also are provided for having some of the great hymns of the church first used and perhaps memorized in the Junior Department, and then used in the Sunday church service.

Children's Choirs

Not to be overlooked is the importance of children's choirs. This gives many of the children in the congregation a definite participation in the worship of God. It is not possible within the limits of this book to do more than to point out the values which come to the entire congregation when the voices of children are lifted in praise to the heavenly Father. The voices of singing children welcomed Christ, one remembers, on that triumphant Palm Sunday so long ago. There is reason to believe that children's voices singing the praises of God find a response not only on earth but also in heaven.

It sometimes happens, of course, that not all the children can be brought into the choir. One must consider, therefore, the children who are left out of the choir because of inability to join in the choir training. Happy is the pastor who has a good children's choir leader and who knows how to make use of the tremendous values of children's choirs!

Variety in Telling the Story

Pastors will vary their methods of telling the junior story sermon. Many pastors call the children to the front pews of the church, when telling the story, in order to give the children a sense of intimacy and friendship with him as the lover of children and as their pastor. In those churches where the children then retire to the Sunday church school, they can usually go quietly from the front pews to the educational building.

Many pastors also feel that in training the children to feel the congeniality of the front pews, they are helping them to avoid, in later life, the habit which seems to possess so many adult worshipers of sitting in the back pews of the church and always avoiding the front pews. The advantage of this is that the pastor has the children's congregation immediately before him rather than talking to them while they are scattered or hidden all over the sanctuary among the adults of the congregation.

On the other hand, many persons feel that the proper place for children is in the pew with their parents where they sense the family relationship throughout the service and where the adults listen to the story with the children in a common interest. Still others feel that coming to the front seats for the story provides a break for the younger children to the monotony of being seated in the pews throughout the service.

Those who desire an even more intimate plan of telling the junior story have adopted the seated chancel steps storytelling method. In the state of New York a famous Presbyterian pastor moves to the upper step of the chancel and invites the children of the congregation to come and seat themselves on the steps. Then he sits on the upper level while they seat themselves on the steps below. In this way, he tells them a brief three-minute story as they look up to him. The method has originality, informality, and even suggestiveness, since it seems to reflect the method which Jesus must often have used in his own teaching. It brings the pastor into very close relationship with his children—a relationship of supreme worth.

Other pastors who prefer an even more informal and intimate method have the seated circle platform story. The children are invited to the carpeted platform and seat themselves in a circle on the floor. Children love to sit on the floor. The pastor, then, either sits in a chair, or if he is sufficiently nimble, he may sit cross-legged on the floor in their midst. This method, perhaps, is suggested by Mark's recital of the parable of the loaves and the fishes when Christ told his disciples to seat the multitude as "flower beds." The gay dresses and bright blouses of children can make a heavenly flower bed on the platform, perhaps adding something of living beauty to the morning worship.

Variety in Method

The minister should vary his methods with the children. It is not always necessary to follow a routine plan. In fact, variety and surprise are important to children. One Sunday a pastor may use the prayer method with his children, another Sunday the hymn method, still another the junior story method. By constantly changing his methods, it will help keep both the children and the congregation alert, and it will also be restful to himself.

Different Types of Stories

The story sermon itself may also have many varied forms. This book contains the typical story, the dramatic story, the missionary story, the biographical story, the object lesson story (without symbolism), stories of Presidents, and stories illustrating doctrinal truths.

A Careful Plan

The pastor who relies mainly on the junior story sermon should carefully plan to maintain variety in the use of his stories. Many pastors during summer vacation think out carefully just the stories and methods to be used each Sunday during the coming year. Some pastors put the planning and outlining of their story sermons for children even before they plan their sermons for the adult congregation. Shocking as this may seem to some people, it is not without some justification. The man who can interest and hold the children of his congregation is not so likely to be unable to hold the adult members in their pews. Few men are condemned because they love children, but many men are blamed because they seem to be indifferent to children and to stand aloof from them.

Other Contacts with Children

These suggestions are not intended to indicate that the worship service is the sole place where a pastor expresses his interest in the children of his church. The Sunday church school is certainly a major place for the expression of his interest and should command the minister's best thinking and planning. Then, too, he will not forget the vacation church school, and he will have regard to his camping program. His parish visitation should always include special attention to the children. He may plan weekday services for the children of his church. Besides all this, he will surely arrange for the pastor's class for those who are to be instructed in the meaning of church membership.

This book, however, is concerned mainly to give help for the pastor's work with the children during the Sunday morning worship.

attention to the children of your congregation pays dividends

"I COULD WEEP," said a visiting English clergyman, "to see the way children are ignored in many of your American worship services."

For years as a guest preacher in one thousand different pulpits across our country, I have been appalled while waiting in the pastor's study for the morning worship service to begin. Looking out the study window I saw the huge parade of boys and girls and young people marching away from the church at the close of the Sunday church school. At the moment the great organ prelude was sounding the call to worship into the house of God, all the church children and young people were marching away from the church posthaste! During these conditioning years, we have been drilling children to march away from the morning worship service. We teach them to leave it behind as not for them.

Years later the church wakes up and asks, "Where are all our young people? Why aren't they in the church worship this morning?"

The answer should be a very simple one: "Why should they be there? When did you train them to attend morning worship?"

Probably you trained them to walk away from the church. When they think they have outgrown the Sunday school, they continue to stay away from church worship. They never have been initiated into the plan of attending morning church worship. The children grow up leaving church worship outside of their practical experience, with

18

the result that when they have finished with the Sunday church school they go out into the world without any well-established custom of church attendance.

There is ample proof that the pastor who is concerned with this problem, and who initiates the family pew or the junior story sermon or some special plan for integrating his children into church worship and for making the experience meaningful to them, is the pastor who is building his worshiping congregation for tomorrow. He will know the delight of seeing these young people grow up without the need of making some violent change in order to attend morning worship. Church attendance will be a plan to which they will have become long accustomed and which will be firmly rooted in their Lord's Day experience. Having pursued this plan during a series of early years when they were adjusting to life, they will grow into the adult congregation in sympathetic participation in all its worship.

What an indescribable tragedy that we should be training children to neglect the very objective for which the church edifice has been erected, and for which it holds open its doors, namely, the worship and praise of God! It is fallacious to say, "We have a strong Sunday school program and we have hundreds of children enrolled in our Sunday school." The question is: "Are they in your church? Are they in your service of worship? Are they being integrated habitually into your morning worship? Will you hold them to the churches when they think their Sunday school days are over?"

Attention to the Children of Your Congregation Pays Dividends

the pastor's children's prayer

MANY BUSY PASTORS, not wanting to carry the burden of a new children's story every Sunday, and desiring to vary their ministry to the children of the congregation, during the worship service offer a brief prayer with the children.

For example, the pastor steps down from the pulpit or chancel, inviting the children to meet him at the front of the sanctuary. He invites them, extending his arms like a shepherd calling his lambs. The children come one by one or in groups down the aisles reverently and quietly until they make a close-knit group in front of the pastor. Still extending his arms around the children, the pastor invites the adult congregation to bow their heads with the children while he offers a prayer in language most easily understood by boys and girls.

This children's prayer will be brief, simple, sincere and understandable by children. The pastor will give thanks for the children's presence in the church. His prayer will make them aware that Jesus loves children and calls them to him. The prayer will take account of the concerns and experiences of children, lifting up before God their praises and petitions in such a way that they can enter into the spirit and understanding of the prayer.

After this prayer has ended many pastors dismiss the children and they go quietly into the educational building for the extended class and study sessions. In other churches the children return to the family pews and remain throughout the service with their parents or friends.

The pastor's prayers with children in this book are intended only to be suggestive. Some of them are grouped around seasons or anniversaries. Others may be used on any Sunday of the year.

children's hymns for morning worship

IT IS SUPREMELY important that children be given a sense of "belong-ingness" in the morning worship, not only by such means as the family pew and the junior story sermon, but also by participation in the musical worship. Sharing in the musical worship may be done through the children's choir, but since many children are not in this choir, the use of a children's hymn by the entire congregation becomes a sure way of including all the children.

Many of the denominational hymnbooks now definitely include a section called "Children's Hymns." In *The Hymnal* of the Presby-terian Church in the United States of America, for example, eighteen hymns are listed in the hymnbook for children, numbers 441-458. Included here are such lovely hymns as "Angel Voices, Ever Singing," by Pott and Sullivan, "I Think When I Read That Sweet Story of Old," by Jemima Luke and sung to the traditional English melody, the lovely hymn, "Savior, Like a Shepherd Lead Us," sung to the Sicilian Mariners' Air, and "I Love to Tell the Story of Unseen Things Above," by Hankey and Fischer.

Hymns of lively interest for children are "Praise Him! Praise Him!" by the blind poet, Fanny J. Crosby, and "Brightly Gleams Our Banner, Pointing to the Sky," by Potter and Sullivan.

Of course, all children should have the opportunity to join in the singing of the Crusader's hymn, "Fairest Lord Jesus," and "Joyful,

21

Joyful, We Adore Thee," written by Henry van Dyke and sung to the strains of Beethoven's "Ninth Symphony."

The new hymnal published jointly by the Presbyterian Church in the United States, the Presbyterian Church in the United States of America, the United Presbyterian Church of North America, and the Reformed Church in America, now widely coming into use in these denominations, has a delightful selection of children's hymns, numbered from 456 to 467.

In the hymnal of the Methodist Church a children's section is numbered from 434 to 457.

Among the selections one finds Charles Wesley's lovely hymn, "Gentle Jesus, Meek and Mild." Another fascinating children's hymn too often omitted from hymnbooks today is "I am so glad that our Father in heaven Tells of his love in the Book he has given," by Oakey and Bliss. One is not surprised, of course, to find for Christmastide "Away in a Manger," and one is pleased to find for springtime "The May Song," by Christina Rossetti, set to a traditional English tune. The ever-moving hymn, "I Think When I Read That Sweet Story of Old," is also included along with the sparkling marching song, "Brightly Gleams Our Banner," by Potter and Sullivan. "Hushed Was the Evening Hymn," by Burns and Sullivan is another hymn most suitable for singing by children.

A pastor may also decide that hymns not listed in the children's section of the hymnbook can be adapted to the understanding of children and can be made meaningful worship to them by his interpretation before the hymn is sung. He may explain some words in the hymn, or he may call attention to one of the verses and ask the children in the congregation to read or recite it. This is a very helpful method, not requiring too much preparation on the part of the pastor, but integrating the children's participation in the worship in such a way that the entire congregation shares by singing the children's hymn. This method also educates the children and indeed the adults in the hymnology of the church.

A new appreciation of the Bible may be gained for the children in the congregation by the singing of the hymn, "Thy Word Is Like a Garden, Lord," by Hodder and Poole. So also Cecil F. Alexander's beautiful hymn, "There Is a Green Hill Far Away," or Stocking's hymn, "O Master Workman of the Race," are of value to boys and girls. Christmas hymns are always a peculiar joy to children. Surely they must have opportunity to sing Martin Luther's "Away in a

Manger," and his ever beautiful hymn, though less well known, "Ah, Dearest Jesus, Holy Child." All the Christmas hymns, because of the widespread musical celebration of the day, are somewhat familiar to children and enjoyed by them. This may be less true of the Easter hymns, but the children should certainly be initiated into the singing of some of the great hymns which celebrate this event.

Of course, there are two great favorite processional hymns which children always love: "Rejoice, Ye Pure in Heart," by Plumtre, and "Onward, Christian Soldiers," by Baring-Gould.

The Disciples of Christ and the American Baptists in their joint hymnbook, *Christian Worship,* list eighty hymns for use with children nine to twelve years of age. They have starred a little over a third of these hymns as suitable for processionals:

*All Beautiful the March of Days
*All Creatures of Our God and King
*All Glory, Laud, and Honor
 As with Gladness Men of Old
 Away in a Manger
 Book of Grace and Book of Glory
*Christ the Lord Is Risen Today
*Come, Thou Almighty King
*Come, Ye Thankful People, Come
*Fairest Lord Jesus
 Faith of Our Fathers
 Father, Loving Father
*Fling Out the Banner
*For the Beauty of the Earth
*Forward Through the Ages
 God of the Earth, the Sky, the Sea
 God Speaks to Us in Bird and Song
 God That Madest Earth and Heaven
 God Who Touchest Earth with Beauty
*Hark! the Herald Angels Sing
*Holy, Holy, Holy! Lord God Almighty
 How Strong and Sweet My Father's Care
 Hush, All Ye Sounds of War
*I Love Thy Kingdom, Lord
 I Love to Tell the Story
 I Think When I Read That Sweet Story of Old

I Would Be True
In Christ There Is No East or West
It Came Upon the Midnight Clear
Jesus Shall Reign Where'er the Sun
*Joy to the World! the Lord Is Come
Joyful, Joyful We Adore Thee
Just as I Am, Thine Own to Be
*Lead On, O King Eternal
Lord of All Being, Throned Afar
Lord, Thy Glory Fills the Heaven
Lord, While for All Mankind We Pray
*Marching with the Heroes
*Men and Children Everywhere
My Country Is the World
My Country, 'tis of Thee
My God, I Thank Thee, Who Hast Made
My Master Was a Worker
*Now in the Days of Youth
Now Praise We Great and Famous Men
Now Thank We All Our God
Now the Day Is Over
O Beautiful for Spacious Skies
*O Come, All Ye Faithful
O Father, Thou Who Givest All
O God, Beneath Thy Guiding Hand
O God, Our Help in Ages Past
O Happy Home, Where Thou Art Loved the Dearest
O Little Town of Bethlehem
O Master Workman of the Race
*O Worship the King, All-glorious Above
*O Zion, Haste
Our Church Proclaims God's Love and Care
*Praise to God, Immortal Praise
Rejoice, Ye Pure in Heart
Remember All the People
Saviour, Teach Me Day by Day
Silent Night, Holy Night
Tell Me the Stories of Jesus
That Cause Can Neither Be Lost nor Stayed
*The Church's One Foundation

The Fathers Built This City
*The Wise May Bring Their Learning
There's a Song in the Air
*This Is My Father's World
To All the Nations, Lord
We Give Thee But Thine Own
We Plow the Fields and Scatter
We Three Kings of Orient Are
*We've a Story to Tell to the Nations
*When Morning Gilds the Skies
When Spring Unlocks the Flowers
While Shepherds Watched Their Flocks by Night
*Wise Men Seeking Jesus
*With Happy Voices Ringing

*Children's
Hymns for
Morning
Worship*

correlating with the sunday church school

THE PASTOR, by correlating his church worship ministry to his children with the worship and study of the Junior Department of the Sunday church school, can greatly enhance the worship experiences of his children. Every pastor wants the children of the congregation to feel at home in the atmosphere of church worship, and to recognize many parts of the worship service as words, phrases, and ideas with which the children are already familiar. Church worship may not be meaningful to a child if all is strange and unfamiliar.

By co-ordinated planning with the Sunday church school, the child can be given new meaning in worship and a real sense of participation. Effective co-ordination can easily be secured if the pastor elicits the co-operation of the junior superintendent and teachers through personal conference with them.

Let the pastor explore a plan for agreeing in advance that he will use in church worship:

1. *Calls to Worship* to be first used for a month or longer in the Junior Department worship of the Sunday church school.

2. *A Worship Hymn* similarly first sung several times and explained in the Sunday church school.

3. *A Scripture Lesson* which will be one of the Scripture passages chosen to be memorized in the Junior Department. Then let him

invite the juniors as a choral-speaking choir or group to give this reading to the Scripture passage in the morning church worship. This he can substitute occasionally for his own reading of the Scripture and thus permit the children to have a share in leading the congregational worship.

4. *An Offering Response* with which the juniors have become familiar in Sunday church school.

5. *A Benediction* first used in the Sunday church school, and adopted by the pastor for his benediction.

In thus using in the morning church worship Scripture sentences and hymns around which the child has had meaningful experiences in Junior Department worship, the pastor will cause the children's faces to glow, their eyes to shine, and their spirits to respond with a sense of belongingness when they participate in the church worship.

Below are offered suggested resources for use in these five methods of correlated worship planning.

Calls to Worship

Make a joyful noise unto the Lord, all ye lands.
Serve the Lord with gladness:
Come before his presence with singing. (Psalm 100:1-2)

The Lord is in his holy temple:
Let all the earth keep silence before him. (Habakkuk 2:20)

O give thanks unto the Lord; call upon his name:
Make known his deeds among the people.
Sing unto him, sing psalms unto him:
Talk ye of all his wondrous works.
Glory ye in his holy name. (Psalm 105:1-3*a*)

O magnify the Lord with me,
And let us exalt his name together. (Psalm 34:3)

Give unto the Lord,
O ye kindreds of the people,
Give unto the Lord glory and strength.
Give unto the Lord the glory due unto his name:
Bring an offering, and come into his courts.
O worship the Lord in the beauty of holiness. (Psalm 96:7-9*a*)

O come, let us worship and bow down:
Let us kneel before the Lord our maker.
For he is our God; and we are the people
Of his pasture, and the sheep of his hand. (Psalm 95:6-7*a*)

I was glad when they said unto me,
Let us go into the house of the Lord.   (Psalm 122:1)

O come, let us sing unto the Lord:
Let us make a joyful noise to the rock of our salvation.
                                        (Psalm 95:1-2*a*)

Let the words of my mouth,
And the meditation of my heart,
Be acceptable in thy sight, O Lord,
My strength, and my redeemer. (Psalm 19:14)

Hymns of the Church to Be Used Both in Junior Worship and Church Worship

> Come, Ye Thankful People, Come
> O God, Our Help in Ages Past
> America the Beautiful
> Holy, Holy, Holy, Lord God Almighty
> The Church's One Foundation
> O Worship the King
> Joyful, Joyful, We Adore Thee
> Rejoice, Ye Pure in Heart
> Fairest Lord Jesus

Offering Responses
The Doxology:

> Praise God, from whom all blessings flow;
> Praise him, all creatures, here below;
> Praise him above, ye heavenly host;
> Praise Father, Son, and Holy Ghost.

The Gloria:

> Glory be to the Father, and to the Son, and to the Holy
> Ghost:

As it was in the beginning,
Is now, and ever shall be,
World without end, Amen.

All things come of Thee, O Lord,
And of Thine own have we given Thee.

We give Thee but Thine own,
Whate'er the gift may be:
All that we have is Thine alone,
A trust, O Lord, from Thee.

Scripture Passages to Be Memorized

> Psalms 1, 23, 24, 103:1-13, 121
> Isaiah 55
> Exodus 20:1-17
> Matthew 5:1-12
> Matthew 28:19-20 (The Great Commission)
> Matthew 16:15-16 (The Great Confession)
> Matthew 22:37-39 (The Two Great Commandments)
> John 3:16 (The Little Gospel)
> I Corinthians 13

Benedictions

> The Lord bless you and keep you;
> The Lord make his face to shine upon you
> And be gracious unto you;
> The Lord lift up his countenance upon you,
> And give you peace.

hints on how to tell your junior stories

THE CHILDREN'S STORY is a serious part of the worship. It should not be regarded as a light moment of entertainment to appease restless children or to relieve tired parents. It should be an integral part of Christian worship, whether in church, Sunday church school, or vacation church school.

While the stories must carry some dignity and conviction, this does not mean that they must always exclude humor and never have touches of bright human situations. The stories must, however, conform to the spirit of children in the morning worship.

The Story Message for Children Requires Special Attention. Doubtless the reason why some congregations have not reacted favorably to the pastor's children's sermon, is because it often simply is not a children's sermon story. It is a story told in the language of adults to adults. The art of storytelling for children is indeed an art.

Use Simple, Short Words. Many a pastor falls down because he uses the same vocabulary with the children that he would use in his adult sermon and he never relaxes from the grip of his theological terminology. As a consequence, the children's story sermon is something endured and often disliked, since it becomes a pathetic failure with the children not entranced.

Write Out Your Story. The wise pastor will write out his children's story sermon. He will watch his words to make sure that they are words that lie within the understanding and the experience of children. The idea that just anybody can tell a children's story or that anything goes with children is colossally false. Children have their own language, their own love of words, and if the storyteller chooses to ignore their desires, the children will reward him by ignoring his effort at storytelling.

Make the Story Brief. The length of the story should be a definite concern. The ideal time limit is three and one-half minutes, though often it may be extended to five or six minutes.

Remember that children have learned to turn off their minds at the end of six or seven minutes just as effectively as they have learned to shut off the radio or television. It is the easiest thing in the world for children to turn off their minds and they may turn them off on your story, if it is too long or dull.

For young children the attention span is very limited. In the morning congregation, however, there is a fairly wide age range. Consequently, a pastor may from time to time vary the length of his children's story. He can aim generally at three and one-half minutes. Where the story requires it or the service permits he may run to five minutes or slightly longer. Brevity is the soul of wit in a children's story. In a service of morning worship much must be packed into an all-too-brief hour of worship.

Avoid the Application. The pastor must avoid another fault which he falls into easily in a children's story. He has been trained homiletically to apply his sermon and to make a part of his sermon a practical application of truth. In telling a children's story, however, he must assiduously avoid making any application of his story. If he tacks on a moral at the end of a story, saying, "Now this story means that, whenever you do thus and so, this and that will happen," then he has robbed the story of its fascination for the children. Actually, he has presented them with an anticlimax that lets them down. If the story does not within itself suggest its own meaning, then it probably is not the best story for children.

Children are keener than we suppose. If they remember the story, its meaning will somehow grow upon them. Mystery and subtlety add to the charm of the tale. Children will make their own application. Many of the parables of Jesus were not immediately apparent in their meaning and even now we are only beginning to grasp their full meaning. Rest content, therefore, with an effective story. If not in the immediate service, then sometime later a remembered story will become the source of full meaning in the life of the growing child.

A somewhat contrary view was recently expressed by Dr. Ernest E. Ligon at a conference at the University of Michigan. Tests made by him show that juniors may get thirteen different ideas of what a story was intended to teach. Tests show that reactions are so vague and varied, Dr. Ligon holds, that the moral should be made unmistakable in the story or its application. "If you want them to get the moral, put it in," says Dr. Ligon. Perhaps he is right.

Don't Talk Down to Children. It is also important not to talk down to the children, but to talk on their level. This is the advantage gained when the pastor seats himself with the children on the same level and somehow avoids talking down to them from the pulpit. Children have their own insights "for of such is the kingdom of heaven" and "angels do always behold the face of my Father which is in heaven." We must respect the intelligence of a child and treat him with all the courtesy, respect, and honor due him as an individual. He does not want baby talk!

Let the Children Laugh. There is a good opportunity for the play of humor in children's stories. Don't miss giving the children a chance to smile in the house of God. The church must be a happy place. Surely Jesus must have loved the laughter of little children.

Stories Must Vie with Children's Interests and Experiences. It must also be remembered that it is very difficult within the average brief story to teach the great theological doctrines. Surprisingly, many of the parables of Jesus apply to human conduct rather than to great doctrines. The story of the good Samaritan, of the talents, the parable of the mustard seed, the parable of the last judgment and others relate to conduct and attitudes of heart and mind rather than to the great theological doctrines of the Incarnation, Revelation, Atonement, and Resurrection. One must not strain a story, therefore, to portray a great doctrine if the story does not lend itself to such presentation. And neither must one be disturbed if there are but few stories available that adequately set forth profound theological doctrines.

The Story Is for the Children. The story, of course, must always be planned for the children and pointed definitely to the children. Nevertheless, it is possible to have overtones in a story which may have meaning for parents and other adult members of the congregation. This double use makes the story a family story where both child and adults share the joy of the story together. Still the story sermon is primarily for the enjoyment of children.

A good story may have overtones, and the overtones may justifiably have a message for the congregation. Indeed there are those rare occasions when a pastor has an unacceptable truth to present to his adult congregation. There may be times when he may make this truth more easily accepted by the means of a children's story. The adult congregation will accept with grace the point of truth in this way which they might resent if it were presented in a hard preachment. Nevertheless, the children's story should never be sabotaged or prostituted to the use of whacking the adult congregation over the head. It must always remain a children's story.

Hints on How to Tell Your Junior Stories

33

CHAPTER 7

create your own children's stories

WHILE THE STORIES in this book are presented as helpful aids to the pastor, it is hoped that they may be suggestive of ways by which the minister may discover and create his own junior story sermons. By watching his own daily experiences, a pastor may come to discover human situations and anecdotes which, mixed with a little imagination, may have meaning for children. Remember that stories may be simple and yet interest a child. If the experience has occurred during the week in his pastoral ministry, it will be told with an immediacy of local color and vividness which will give it a rare freshness of appeal.

For example, he may have observed a blind man being led along the way by a Seeing Eye dog. He may have noticed the earnestness and fidelity of the dog to his blind master. He may have noticed how the dog looked in all directions at crossings, how the dog pulled on his harness in order to steer his master around the corner. He may have observed the patience of the dog quietly waiting when his master had to remain seated during a long service. In many ways, the pastor can make a graphic story out of just this experience for the boys and girls of his congregation.

Or he may have taken a trip in an airplane. A story may come out of his experiences at the airport where he saw the big super-six-engine planes that go 400 miles an hour and carry 150 passengers.

34

At the same airport, he may have seen a tiny, little one-engine plane or a small helicopter. His imagination can create a conversation between the little one-engine plane and the giant six-engine plane. The conversation could show how important a small plane can be when the pilot gets in and has his hand at the controls. He might even make a story about the giant plane running into a storm and how the pilot zooms his plane up and up above the storm clouds into the serene sunshine.

In everyday human experiences there are fascinating situations of perennial interest to the children. They love trains, airplanes, animals, fire engines, and babies. Contacts the pastor has with these things can always be made into interesting stories to tell to his children.

A minister may look around his church at his stained-glass windows. There may be stories in his windows. He can give a talk on each window or tell the Bible story presented in each window. This will give new meaning to the children's experience of worship in the church. Children can be helped to understand the Christian symbols displayed about the church, for they already know that the flag is the symbol of our country. Where is the child who does not understand that the Valentine heart stands for friendship and love? Even $2 + 2 = 4$ are symbols learned early in life. The cross, the Christian flag, the Bible, the baptistry, the Triangle, the Alpha and Omega, I.N.R.I., and the Circle may all be explained by the pastor in story form.

One well-known pastor who has served more than fifty years in his church has had notable success in his cultivation of children in his congregation. He invites a group of children into the front pews, having given them, a week beforehand, a verse of Scripture which they are to read the following Sunday in the service when called upon by the pastor. He then calls upon a few of them by name to read the assigned verse of Scripture. He encourages them to tell him and the congregation in their own words what they think the verse means. Their interpretations often show rare spiritual insight, though sometimes they may be amusing, and often they require help from the pastor in order that the verse may be made clear to them. This is useful in congregations where biblical training is held to be of first importance and undoubtedly has special values in training children in their appreciation of the Bible and its meaning. This method displaces the need for giving a junior story sermon, for the children themselves, as they participate, are really acting out a story.

Object Stories

May object stories be used? Yes, if they are not used symbolically. An effective Thanksgiving junior sermon can be made out of simple objects which can be shown to the children with a pointed comment on how grateful we ought to be to possess the object, and how poor and frustrated we would be without these objects. For example, a salt shaker may be used to show how flat our Thanksgiving potatoes, squash, turnips, and turkey would all be if we had no salt to make our food palatable. An eraser may be shown with the remark that we would all be unhappy if we could not erase something we had written or correct a mistake we have made.

A postage stamp may be shown on a letter indicating the pleasure we receive from our ability to place a stamp on a letter and send an invitation to our friends to come to Thanksgiving dinner, or receive from them through the mail a promise that they are coming to share Thanksgiving with us. We can think behind the postage stamp to all the air mail planes and trains and the mail trucks and the letter carriers, the red, white, and blue mail boxes, and all that the stamp represents. How thankful we should be for just the use of postage stamps!

A toy telephone may be taken into the pulpit expressing our gratitude that we are able to telephone our friends far, far away and hear their voices and send a Thanksgiving message to them on the wire, or just a yellow telegram blank may be used instead of a telephone to show the same thing. A clock or a watch may be shown indicating how thankful we should be that we know the time when school closes, the time to come to church on Sunday morning, when it is getting time for our Thanksgiving dinner, and many other uses all which we owe to the faithful clock or watch. How very poor we would be without a timepiece!

A large calendar might be shown with Thanksgiving Day marked in red indicating how thankful we are that we can know the months and the day when Thanksgiving arrives. An electric light bulb may be shown and it may be attached in order to switch on the light indicating how very dark our homes would be and how black and lonely the night, if we could not turn on the electric light. The New Testament might be held up with the comment that we could be utterly poor if we did not have the life of Jesus and the story of his death and resurrection. We can point out how thankful we ought to be that we have reason to give thanks to God on Thanksgiving Day, not only for the blessings of home and food and friends and family, but also for the great blessing for our eternal Friend, our Savior and Redeemer, the Lord Jesus Christ.

Such a simple series of objects held up very briefly with terse comment can make an apt story on Thanksgiving Sunday when a similar use of objects might fall flat on some other Sunday. By using these objects with the Thanksgiving theme, however, the illustration can be very effective, not only for the children but also for the adult congregation.

In the springtime of the year, a pastor may make an effective use of an object if he will go into his garden and very carefully dig up a weed, preserving its long, long root system. If in first presenting these two objects he will conceal the roots from the children, and then show how the weed extends its roots and takes away strength and nourishment from the flower, he can give children a vivid awareness of the danger of evil associations growing strong. But he can give the object talk a positive side by showing the strength and beauty of flowers whose roots are allowed to grow without losing strength to weeds.

As another device using an object in a non-symbolic way, the pastor may hold in his hand a silver dollar, half dollar, quarter, dime, nickel, or penny. He may even ask the children to look at the coins they may have in their pockets. He may invite them to read in concert with him the phrase inscribed on each coin, "In God We Trust." He can point out how this first came to be inscribed on our coins during the War Between the States at the suggestion made to Secretary of the Treasury Chase by a Methodist minister in Ridley, Pennsylvania. He can go on to point out that this same sentence is inscribed now on the dollar bill and on a special three-cent stamp. The pastor should then explain the meaning of this inscription with some words about the religious background of our nation.

In the spring of the year the pastor may use some rosebuds. He can show why it is not wise to pick open the bud or help the rose to bloom more quickly by our impatient and premature opening of the petals by hand. He can show how the bud must be allowed to grow, responding to the sunshine and rain and the warmth of springtime and the power of God. He can help boys and girls not to be impatient, but to take time to study and to let their muscles and minds and bodies grow according to God's plan and God's beautiful

37

laws of growth. By showing how the forcing of rosebuds unnaturally only hurts the blossom, so we can also help parents of children to be patient and wait for God's laws of growth.

Other objects can be used by pastors if they are careful not to use symbolism in connection with the objects, since young children for the most part have difficulty in grasping the meaning of the symbol. Other subjects which may be used are strips of colored ribbons as Bible bookmarks, which may, on rare occasions, be given to the children; smooth beach pebbles which the minister has collected on his vacation; some Perry pictures; Christmas and Easter cards; bright colored pencils; valentines; colored autumn leaves; tinsel Christmas stars; and a host of other inexpensive objects.

Objects should be used with great restraint, and the giving of objects to the children should be done only rarely, for there is always the danger that they may be conditioned into thinking the church is a place where one collects objects and souvenirs rather than a house of God where one worships. On the other hand, from time to time children will welcome a gift however small, and no pastor can forget the words of John Masefield:

> He who gives a child a treat
> Makes joy bells ring in Heaven's streets.

Using Art Masterpieces

A pastor may choose to introduce his children to some of the masterpieces of Christian art. If he lives near a large city, he can have a photostatic blowup made of an art picture large enough to be seen all over the sanctuary. He should have it veiled until the proper time in the morning service. Then, while the organ plays very soft music, he can tell the story of the picture. In this way, he could deal with pictures like Plockhorst's "Christ Blessing Little Children," "The Lost Sheep," by Soord, and a host of other religious masterpieces.

This will be a new idea to many pastors, but for a relatively small expense children may be trained in appreciation of Christian art, a neglected training. It also trains the adult congregation in the appreciation of some of the great religious masterpieces.

The expense of making the blowups is not great, if a pastor were to do them say one Sunday out of a month, or ten great masterpieces a year. The pictures can be blown up on heavy material like masonite, so they can easily be made to stand up in the chancel or pulpit. If there is anyone in the congregation who is an artist or deft with colors, these black-and-white blowups can be colored to resemble the great originals. We recommend this as a very serious plan of enhancing worship values and the art appreciation of not only boys and girls but of the entire family of God.

"There is nothing children like better," says a children's expert, "than to feel they are learning something that has value." You may be quite sure they will follow your description of art pictures with glowing satisfaction if, for instance, you use Millet's "The Angelus," and interpret the full meaning of the picture for them.

resource books for good children's stories

THE PASTOR WHO is to minister to his children every Sunday of the year will need to go to a library of good children's storybooks. He will frequently find that only one or two stories in an entire book are usable for his purposes. Yet, if he is successful in getting two or three stories which he can tell his children, he should feel the price of the book is well worth it.

Unfortunately, many good books are out of print and the pastor will have to rely upon a public library. If economy is important and he cannot afford to add too many children's books to his library, he can then borrow a half dozen books from the library and have his secretary, his wife, or his daughter copy out the stories which he selects for his use, thus building his own loose-leaf resource book of stories immediately available to his needs.

We suggest the following resource books:

Bailey, Carolyn Sherwin. *Stories for Sunday Telling.* Pilgrim Press. 1916.

Bays, Alice A. *Worship Programs and Stories for Young People.* Abingdon. 1938.

Bouve, Pauline Carrington. *Lamp-light Tales.* Grosset and Dunlap. 1922.

Brown, Jeanette Perkins. *The Storyteller in Religious Education.* Pilgrim Press. 1951.

Bryant, Sara Cone. *How to Tell Stories to Children*. Houghton Mifflin. 1905.

Bryant, Sara Cone. *Stories to Tell to Children*. Houghton Mifflin. 1907.

Eggleston, Margaret W. *Forty Stories for the Church, School and Home*. Harper. 1939.

Farrar, James M. *A Junior Congregation*. Funk and Wagnalls. 1910.

Fischbach, Julius. *Children's Sermons in Stories*. Abingdon. 1955.

Fischbach, Julius. *Story Sermons for Boys and Girls*. Abingdon-Cokesbury. 1947.

Gates, Sherwood. *Junior Church Manual*. Harper. 1929.

Herzberg and Momes. *Americans in Action*. D. Appleton-Century. 1917.

Kelsey, Alice Geer. *Stories for Junior Worship*. Abingdon-Cokesbury. 1954.

Kelsey, Alice Geer. *Story Sermons for Juniors*. Abingdon-Cokesbury. 1953.

Kerr, Hugh T. *Children's Story Sermons*. Fleming H. Revell. 1911.

Kerr, Hugh T. *Children's Nature Story-Sermon*. Fleming H. Revell. 1923.

Lantz, J. Edward. *Best Religious Stories*. Association Press. 1948.

Lantz, J. Edward. *Stories of Christian Living*. Association Press. 1950.

Lindsay, Maud. *The Story-teller*. Lothrop, Lee and Shepard. 1915.

Millen, Nina. *Missionary Hero Stories*. Friendship Press. 1948.

Millen, Nina. *The Missionary Story Hour*. Friendship Press. 1952.

Missionary Stories to Tell. Friendship Press. 1937.

More Missionary Stories to Tell. Friendship Press. 1941.

Morgan, Walter Amos. *The Dreams of Youth*. Century. 1928.

Odell, Mary C. *Another Story Shop*. Judson Press. 1947.

Odell, Mary C. *The Story Shop*. Judson Press. 1938.

Olcutt, Frances Jenkins. *Good Stories for Anniversaries*. Houghton Mifflin. 1937.

Patton, Carl S. *Two Minute Stories*. Willett, Clark, and Colby. 1930.

Sadler, Alfred J. *Story Sermons for Juniors*. Abingdon. 1923.

Smith, Jean Louise. *Great Art and Children's Worship*. Abingdon-Cokesbury. 1948.

Whitehouse, Elizabeth S. *Kingdom Stories for Juniors*. Fleming H. Revell. 1928.

stories for any time

A SELFISH GULL

(A story showing selfishness to be self-defeating)

DOT AND BILL were eating their picnic lunch on the high rocks overlooking the Atlantic Ocean down near their cottage in Maine, where they were spending their summer holidays. It was a hot July day, but the ocean breeze was so cool, and the air so salty and full of tang.

"Dot, see that big wave coming in!" Bill shouted, as a huge breaker dashed upon the rocks below them and shot a column of beautiful white spray high into the air.

"I just love to watch the tide coming in. See how it is creeping up on these rocks!" said Dot.

"Yes," rejoined Bill. "You can tell that the tide is rising because the rocks are getting wet higher up all the time."

Suddenly Dot pointed up over her head and asked, "Oh, why are those white sea gulls flying in circles around us?"

"They are flying around expecting to get our leftover lunch, of course," answered Bill.

"Is that why they are all making those shrill cries of 'Kullah, Kullah, Kullah'?" asked Dot.

"Sure," said Bill. "They are excited, they are hungry, and they are calling their friends to come. It sounds to me as if they are calling, 'Hurry, Hurry, Hurry.'"

Many gulls were flocking around. As they floated lazily above Dot and Bill, they craned their necks, cocked their heads, and fixed their beady eyes on the lunch being munched below.

"Well, I'm full already," said Dot. "Mother prepared too many sandwiches for me. I can't eat all of them."

"I'm full, too," said Bill. "I know what, let's take a few of these sandwich scraps and put them in a little pile on the rocks for the gulls to eat for their lunch. Then we can watch the whole flock of

43

gulls swoop down and eat. It'll be fun seeing them poke their bills into the food." And with that, Bill and Dot gathered up the bits of leftover sandwiches and set up the gulls' lunch on the rocks just a little above the line that the ocean's rising tide had then reached.

Almost instantly, several gulls swooped down toward the food, with one big gull leading all the others. The big, old gull flew so fast that he got to the food first. As the other gulls flew near, he began to attack them with his bill and drive them away. It was perfectly clear that this big, old, selfish gull intended to have all those delicious sandwiches himself.

"Oh, look at that selfish bully," said Dot. "He won't share one crumb of those sandwiches. Just because he's bigger and bolder does not give him any right to act so selfish. For all he's so good-looking he really is hateful!"

Dot and Bill watched the other gulls. One by one, first on one side, then on the other, they would alight on the rocks near the food; then they would start walking over toward the lunch which Bill and Dot had put there for them all. But the selfish gull would savagely drive them off, spreading his wings wide and opening his bill threateningly, as if he would bite them. So they did not dare to come close enough to get any food.

In fact, the selfish gull had no time to get at the lunch himself. The other hungry gulls kept worrying the bully by creeping nearer and nearer the food. The selfish gull kept getting angrier and angrier because it was so much work to keep driving off the gulls in order to protect the sandwich bits all for himself alone. He just had no time to stop and eat. He began to pant for breath. It was dash here at a gull coming in front of him, now dash at a gull creeping up behind him, now attack that gull to the right of him, now fly against the gull to the left of him, until he was almost beside himself trying to make his mean, old, selfish plan work—his plan not to share one bit of food with friend or foe.

In fact, the selfish gull was so frantically busy with his selfishness that he did not notice one very important thing. He had forgotten the mighty ocean and the powerful waves. The tide was rising, and the waves were coming closer and closer to the lunch. He did not notice that just about one more wave would reach the place where he was defending the food.

Just as the selfish gull made one last dash to drive away another hungry brother gull, a big wave came along, lifted the pieces of food off the rocks, and, with a great swoosh, floated and tossed the sandwich bits all over the blue waves. Instantly the whole flock of gulls swooped down on the floating food—scores of them. In split seconds every scrap of the lunch disappeared.

Now the selfish gull returned from driving away that last brother gull. He came back to the high rocks feeling very triumphant as if to say, "Ah, now I will gorge myself on the lunch all alone." But you never saw such a bewildered bird in your life. He walked 'round and 'round, up and down the rocks, looking, searching, cawing, calling, and crying, "Kullah, Kullah, Kullah," in the saddest voice you ever heard. To this day, I warrant that selfish old gull doesn't know what happened to his lunch.

But Dot and Bill knew, and they held on to their sides laughing to see the old gull so busy just being selfish, that he never got even the tiniest bite of that lunch for himself.

THE FORGET-ME-NOT

(An imaginative story of how the flowers got their names)

ONE DAY THE heavenly Father gave to the Earth Angel a basket of seeds and said, "Go, plant these seeds beside the brooks and in the fields and woods of the earth to make the earth beautiful and to make the children of the earth happy."

So, as soon as the snow had melted and the earth was warm in the early springtime, the Earth Angel came down on soft wings and scattered the seeds beside the brooks, over the meadows and fields, and in the woods.

"I can hardly wait," the angel said, "to see the tiny seeds sprout and grow into beautiful flowers to make the children of the world happy."

When the flowers were all dressed in their beautiful colors, the heavenly Father said to the Earth Angel, "Go down to earth and give each flower a name. I am sure they are so beautiful they will all want to have a name of their own."

The Earth Angel was so happy to be sent to give names to the pretty flowers. To the big tall flower with the yellow petals and the big brown center the angel said, "Because you look always at the 45 sun, turning all day so as to face it, your name shall be Sunflower."

Then the angel came to a little flower, all gold and shaped like a cup, that was blooming in the meadow. "Why," said the angel, "you look so much like butter that your name shall be Buttercup," and with that all the buttercups began to dance in the soft breeze that rippled across the meadow.

The angel came to another flower whose stem had sharp thorns, but whose beautiful petals were soft as velvet and colored rose like the dawn of the morning. "Because you have thorns but are so beautiful, I shall name you the Rose," said the angel.

So the angel went from flower to flower and gave them lovely names.

At last the angel came to a very tiny flower that was growing beside the brooks and in the meadows and at every corner of the earth. It had tiny blue petals, frail and dainty, each flower with eyes like the blue of the sky, and a heart the color of gold. The angel had to stoop down very low and whisper its name to the tiny, dainty flower.

The angel went back to the heavenly Father and said that now all the flowers had their names. "But what will happen," said the angel, "when the frost kills and the ice and snow fall upon the flowers? I am afraid they will all be killed," said the angel.

So the kind Father in heaven who made the flowers so beautiful said to the angel, "Before the snow and the ice and the frost come you must go down and put the flowers all to sleep in their little beds of earth. You must cover them with pretty blankets of fallen leaves, little patchwork quilts of red and gold, green and brown. Let them rest and sleep through the winter. Then you may wake them in the springtime and let one of each kind of flower come and stand before me and give its name."

In the springtime when the flowers began to awake from their long sleep and to shake their drowsy heads and to get up, putting on their beautiful dresses, the angel came down and said, "The heavenly Father wants to see you. As I present you, you must each give your name."

So the flowers came and the Rose said, "I am the Rose." And the Sunflower said, "I am the Sunflower." And the Buttercup, shiny and gold, said, "I am the Buttercup." But way down the line the little dainty flower with eyes as blue as the sky and heart the color of gold was crying.

46

The other flowers said, "Why are you crying?"

And the tiny blue flower said, "I have forgotten my name! I slept so long I can't even remember my name any more."

"There, there," said the other flowers, "just think hard and perhaps you can remember."

"No, no," cried the little blue flower, "I have been thinking hard all the time, and I just cannot remember what my name is."

Then the angel came and said, "Don't weep any more, little blue flower. If you can't remember your name, the heavenly Father will give you another name and it shall be the most beautiful of all names."

So when the tiny blue flower stood timid and afraid before the heavenly Father, the kindly Father said, "You have forgotten your name, but don't cry. I made you because I wanted you to be beautiful and I wanted you to give beauty to all corners of the earth. 'Forget-me-not' shall be your name. This will help you to remember, for you shall be the tiny blue stars that grow on earth; and up in the sky the shiny gold stars will be 'the forget-me-nots of heaven.' "

(This may be added to the story if the pastor desires.)

Today in our service of worship we observe the Lord's Supper because Jesus our Savior and Lord said to his disciples, "Forget me not. Always do this in remembrance of me." So we may say that this Communion Service today is the request of Jesus, our Great Friend: "Forget me not." If we always remember him, not only in church but in our school and home and play, we can help to make the world beautiful like the meadows filled with the flowers that the angel planted.

WHY THE WORKMEN WORKED

(*Appreciation for the value of work*)

A TRAVELER in a faraway country, as he walked down the road, saw ahead of him in the fields a large number of men busily working. As he walked nearer the men, led on by his curiosity to see what was going on, he saw also a big derrick and great piles of stones, and he heard noises of chiseling, hammering, and pounding.

It was a July day and the hot sun was beating down upon the workmen. Their shoulders were bared to the sun, and the muscles of their arms were tanned to a bronze color. The men were pushing and pulling and struggling. Oxen were pulling huge blocks of stones on carts with big wheels while the men shouted to the slow-moving oxen, "Gee-haw, gee-haw, gee-haw," as they dragged forward the heavy loads. Other men were pounding the stones with great sledge hammers, keeping a kind of rhythmic tune which seemed to sing "zing-ring," "zing-ring," "zing-ring."

Soon the traveler came up to the nearest man who was standing over a block of granite with a hammer in his hand. He also had a very sharp chisel in his left hand.

"Good day, my friend," said the traveler cheerily.

Grumpily the man replied, "Hello, stranger."

The traveler said, "May I ask, my good man, what you are doing here?"

With an unfriendly grunt, the man replied, "Can't you see for yourself I am chipping stone, chipping stone, chipping stone, all day long I am doing nothing but chipping stone, chipping stone, chipping stone, till I'm tired and sick of seeing stones and chips and dust?"

The traveler walked along to another workman, hoping he might find a more friendly person. This man, with the help of other workmen, was lifting heavy stones and loading them into an ox cart. The stones were very heavy for the man to lift, and the muscles of his arms stood out and the muscles of his back were strained. He was perspiring as he groaned and helped to lift the stones in the hot sun.

"May I ask, my good man," said the traveler, trying very hard to be friendly, "what you are doing?"

"Well, if you ask me," said the man in a very harsh voice, "I'm getting some money. At the end of the week, I expect a pay envelope with some money in it. That's what I'm doing, stranger, getting some money, getting some money, getting some money. Does that satisfy you?"

Much disappointed at this unfriendly reply, the weary traveler walked off, still wondering what all this noise, hammering, and chiseling, and all the piles of stones, and the oxen and derricks could be about, and to what purpose.

Finally, the traveler saw a workman who looked as if he had a kind, friendly face. In fact, sometimes he was whistling at his work, and sometimes he was singing a merry tune. "Here is a friendly man who can answer my question," thought the traveler. "May I ask, my good man," he said cheerfully, "what you are doing here?"

"Why, yes," said the workman, "I am proud and happy to tell you. What I am doing here is a wonderful thing. I am building a cathedral for the worship of God. You may think this sounds foolish that I, a single man, am building a cathedral, but all of us working together will soon erect to the praise and glory of God a beautiful temple where many people will come to pray, and where great choirs will sing, and where the organ music will roll through the arches like the sound of a thousand angel wings. Yes, good stranger, I am building a cathedral."

THE QUARREL OF THE PIN FAMILY

(Consideration for the feelings of others)

THE PIN FAMILY had a quarrel. Why such bright, shiny, little Christian pins should quarrel is a mystery! But quarrel they did, in spite of their upbringing and their going to Sunday school. They were doing nothing but looking about the room from their soft cushion in front of the mirror on the bureau, admiring themselves in the looking glass. I think this is where the mischief began, when they were doing nothing.

Darning Needle had come to visit the Pin family, but one of the small Pin sisters, Susan Pin, just didn't like him. Susan Pin said, behind his back, "I'd like to know what that darning needle is good for anyway. Look at him. He hasn't any head on him at all."

Darning Needle overheard what Susan said behind his back, and he sassed her back, "Thank goodness I'm not pin-headed like some folks, and besides, I have a good big eye, and some people who boast about their little heads haven't even got an eye."

So Susan Pin tried to think of something to keep up the quarrel, and she said to her playmates who were around her in the pin cushion, "Darning Needle walks with a stick in his side. Hee, hee, I don't think he will live long, and he can't bend his back without breaking it. He's just one big stiff."

Darning Needle then told his brother Safety Pin that Susan Pin could be as crooked as a bent pin, and that he would rather have a black cat cross his path on Friday the thirteenth than to meet Susan Pin on the street pointing at him. Furthermore, he was so ungentle-

49

manly as to say that if he ever saw her lying on the sidewalk, he would never pick her up. "She would only prick me, if I did," he said.

There was another quarrel between Clothes Pin and Safety Pin. Safety Pin kept saying mean things about Clothes Pin who was lying in a bag hanging over the back of the chair. "Clothes Pin is wooden; he just doesn't have any snap in him."

Then Clothes Pin went around among his friends and told them that Safety Pin was no good unless he was shut up tight; that nobody likes to see a Safety Pin showing anyway.

Clothes Pin then drew himself up very straight and said, "There are always great responsibilities hanging on my line."

"But you are a dumbbell," retorted Safety Pin.

"I am not so sharp as to be always jabbing people and making them cry with pain when I open up," returned Clothes Pin.

Then there was Stick Pin who wore a jewel in his head and was always accused of being stuck up in the chest and always wanting a permanent place. He retaliated by calling all the other pins, "A queer set of pins." In fact, he said, "They are all queer, except me."

Suddenly, the lazy pins on the soft cushion struck right out straight as they heard a deep voice speaking from the direction of the cupboard.

"Good gracious, what self-important, inflated balloons you pins all are! You are simply nobodies, nobodies compared with me. Why, think what I can do! I can flatten out puffed-up pastry, and make crusts for pies, and dough for donuts, and raspberry tarts. I'm the really important pin after all." This was Bully Rolling Pin speaking.

And so the quarrel went on, and it might have continued until this day, had not Mother Smith ended it all in a very quick way.

Mother Smith came rushing in. She put her hands on all the pins and set them all to work. She took Clothes Pin and put him firmly on the line holding up some clothes. Here he had to hold on with both his jaws so tight that he hadn't any chance to quarrel with anybody or to say anything.

Bobby Smith had a button come off his blouse just as he was hurrying to the school bus. So Mother Smith hurriedly fixed it with Safety Pin. This meant that Safety Pin had to go to school with Bobby Smith and stay shut up and perfectly quiet all day long in school.

Mother Smith was short of pins, so she made Stick Pin take the place of Common Pin. She bent Common Pin so he could hold some pieces of cloth together. Then Mother Smith took the Bully Rolling

Pin and made him hustle until he had rolled out enough pastry for a dozen pie crusts, two dozen donuts, and ten apple pies, which kept him so busy he was wet with perspiration and had never a word of boasting to say.

So the quarrel of the Pin family ended, when they all got to work. Whenever you hear the Pin family quarreling, it is a sure sign that they have nothing to do, except think about themselves. For Mother Smith said as she put them all to work, "The devil finds mischief for idle hands. But those who are busy with work have no time to think up mean things to say or do."

THE ALL-BY-MYSELF-ALONE CAKE

(Appreciation for the work of others)

"WALK ON TIPTOE all through the house, Daddy," Wendy demanded of her father in great excitement, as he came in the front door one evening.

"I've got a sponge cake in the oven that I made all-by-myself-alone, Daddy, and please walk on tiptoe or you might make my cake fall. I'm almost ready to take my cake out of the oven and I want you to see my cake. Come right into the kitchen, quick!"

Her father followed Wendy, walking quietly as a kitten. Very softly Wendy opened the oven door and then she screamed with delight. "Oh, my cake is just perfect."

"It is a beautiful cake," said her father.

"Yes," said Wendy, as she carried it carefully to the pantry. "My cake is wonderful and to think that I made this cake all-by-myself-alone! And just think, Daddy, nobody helped me at all."

Her father put an arm about Wendy and gave her a big squeeze. "Your daddy is proud of you," he said. "I can hardly wait to eat some of your cake. I want to have a big piece for dinner."

Susan, who was Wendy's playmate, came over from the next house. Wendy proudly showed her the cake in the pantry.

"What a lovely golden sponge cake!" said Susan.

"Yes," replied Wendy, as she tossed her head into the air. "And I made my cake all-by-myself-alone, and nobody helped me at all."

Susan's brother, John, who seemed to be able to smell cookies and 51 cakes a long way off, came in through the kitchen saying, "Oh, what is that I smell?"

Wendy tilted her head into the air. "Oh, it's just a golden sponge cake that I made all-by-myself-alone, and nobody helped me at all."

At supper Wendy was beaming when her father began to eat a piece of her cake. "This is a very fine cake, Mother," he said.

Wendy looked all around the table, gave her head a little toss, "Yes, I made this cake all-by-myself-alone, and nobody helped me at all."

This time Wendy's father looked across the table at Wendy's mother and then said to Wendy, "So you did it all alone, without help from anyone? How did you know what to put into the cake?" he asked.

"Oh," replied Wendy, "Mother showed me a cake recipe in her big cookbook, the one with the blue covers."

"How many eggs did you use and where did you get them?" her father inquired.

"That's the wonderful part of it," answered Wendy, "I used only ten eggs, those lovely, fresh eggs, you know, that the farmer's wife brings in from the country for Mother every week. I did feel sorry when she brought them to our door yesterday. It was bitterly cold and she looked half-frozen."

"Do you have to use flour in making a cake?" her father pretended ignorance.

"Of course, Daddy," Wendy said. "I used that fine cake flour that Mother buys down at the store, and besides that, we have to use milk and flavoring."

"And did you cook it in the gas oven?" her father questioned.

"Why do you ask so many silly questions about what I put into the cake?" demanded Wendy.

"Well," said her father, "I was trying to figure out how many people really had a hand in making this cake. You said so often that this was an 'all-by-myself-alone' cake. I was thinking of your mother's cookbook, and the one who discovered this recipe, and of the printers who set the type for the cookbook, of the farmer's wife who fed her hens twice a day so that you could have those fine eggs for your cake, and who came to deliver the eggs at our door on the cold winter morning. I was thinking, too, of the farmers who planted the wheat over in Kansas, and of the millers who ground the wheat into flour. I was thinking of the farmer who got up at four o'clock in the morning to milk the cows. I was thinking of the vanilla bean that grows down in the tropics, and the men who extracted the juice to make a flavoring for your cake. I was thinking also of the man shoveling the coal in the boilers of the gas house to provide the cooking gas with which you baked your cake. And really, Wendy, I was beginning to wonder if there could be such a thing as an 'all-by-myself-alone' cake?"

"Daddy, I never thought of that before," responded Wendy slowly. "I had forgotten how much we depend for about everything on other people. I think I must have had a good many hands in my cake bowl, when I was mixing and baking my cake. I didn't know how selfish I was, when I thought that I had made this cake all-by-myself-alone."

"Perhaps we can find a new name for the cake," said her father. "How's this, Wendy—an 'all-by-myself-with-help-from-lots-of-other-people' cake?"

Wendy squealed with delight. "I just love that name; it even sounds like a much nicer cake."

Mother laughed, too, and said, "The Bible has a good verse for your cake-making. Can you guess what it is?"

After a moment, Wendy said, "It must be that one we learned in vacation church school, 'We are laborers together with God.'"

And so it was.

RASPBERRY JAM

(Joyous relief when sin is confessed and forgiven)

THE HOUSE WAS filled with the delicious odors of raspberries, black-berries, and gooseberries cooking on the stove. John's mother had made all kinds of delicious jams. Then she had put them in shiny jelly glasses and arranged them on the pantry shelves, high up where they glistened in rows of red, black, and green.

John's and Mary's mother was very proud of her jams and jellies. As the children watched her store the pretty glass jars of jam on the pantry shelves, she said, "I am so glad we have a good supply of these luscious jellies, and I am counting on you children not to touch them until I am ready to use them. You see, I am saving the jam for Thanksgiving and Christmas." John could not help but feel his mouth water as he looked at the rows of luscious jam jars, but he swallowed hard.

After his mother left the house, however, John kept thinking about

the jam. He liked raspberry jam best of all. He thought that he could climb up on a chair and take just a little bit of jam out of one of the jars and his mother would never know. When he thought his sister was upstairs, he climbed up on a chair in the pantry, but when he got hold of the jam jar, he slipped and the glass fell to the floor and broke into many gooey pieces.

John swept the broken bits of glass into the dustpan the best he could in his hurried fright. He took a paper towel and mopped up the jam from the floor. Then he threw everything into the trash can and put the cover on.

Most unfortunately, as he was cleaning up the jam, his sister Mary appeared in the doorway of the pantry, exclaiming, "Oooh, Mother won't like this, and you will be sorry!"

Of course, as a matter of fact, when his mother came back, she didn't know what had happened, but his sister Mary did know, for she had seen the accident. Everything was serene and she said, "Mary, will you please bring my loafers from my upstairs bedroom?"

"You go, John, and get Mother's loafers," demanded Mary.

"Mother asked you," John retorted.

Then John saw by his sister's eyes that she was signaling him this message! "You know what I know that Mother doesn't know about you."

Quick as a flash, John said, "Never mind, I'll go get the loafers." Mary held her head high in triumph like the young tyrant that she was.

It was about two hours later that their mother said suddenly, "Oh, Mary dear, I am expecting company for dinner tonight. Will you please get the dust cloth and dust the living room for me?"

As it happened, at that moment Mary's head was buried deep in a book she was reading. She quietly lifted her eyes and said to her brother, "John, will you please dust the living room for Mother? I don't want to stop reading my book, for I am at the most interesting part."

John, who hated doing a girl's work, said, "No, I won't. Dusting isn't my job."

Mary fixed her sharp eyes on her brother. They were plainly signaling to him, "You'd better do what I say, because you know what I know that Mother doesn't know about you."

So, with a look of scorn and disgust, John got the dust cloth and dusted the living room. All the time he was dusting, Mary lolled back in the easy chair, reading her book to her heart's content.

Just before dinner Mother said, "Oh, dear, where's the confectioner's sugar? Here I am, ready to frost this cake, and I'm all out of it. Mary, please run to the corner grocery store before it closes and buy me a box of confectioner's sugar."

Without even getting out of the chair, Mary called, "John, John, please go to the store for Mother and get her a box of confectioner's sugar."

John retorted, "Mother didn't ask me to go; she asked you."

This time Mary spoke aloud. "You'd better go and do this for me, John, because you know what I know that somebody doesn't know."

Like a whipped puppy, John had to obey his bossy sister. He was getting mighty tired of letting Mary boss him around just because she knew about his disobedience and the hush-hush accident with the jam.

When John was getting ready for bed that night, something happened that his sister Mary didn't know about. Because John had been so unhappy all day, he went into his mother's room and frankly confessed to her about the broken jar of jam. Of course, John's mother told him she was glad that he had told the truth. She could see that he was sorry and unhappy about the whole thing, and had probably learned his lesson, so she forgave him with a good, big kiss.

The next morning Mary was as haughty as the day before. She had big plans to make John do all her work and run all her errands.

Later that morning, when Mother said, "Mary, will you please come and help me with the dishes?" Mary immediately turned to John and said, "I am tired. I don't like to do the dishes. John, you help Mother with the dishes."

Imagine how surprised and shocked Mary was when John said, "No, I will not!"

Then Mary blazed at him, "You'd better do the dishes, for if you don't, I will tell Mother what I know about you."

John only smiled at Mary. "I have already told her," he said. "She knows all about it and has forgiven me. You can't boss me around any more!"

It was then that John really understood for the first time how true was the memory verse from last Sunday's Sunday school lesson:

> "Blessed [happy] is he whose transgression [sin] is forgiven" (Psalm 32:1).

SIX LITTLE MICE IN A PIANO

(A story introducing the idea of God with overtones for adults)

RICKY, AGED TEN, after family prayers one night said to his grandfather, "Grandpa, you know what a boy in school asked me today?"

"No," said Grandpa, "what did a boy ask you?"

"Of course he knows I go to Sunday school," Ricky replied, "and so he said to me, 'How do you know there is a God when you can't even see him?' and, Grandpa, how do we know that God really is when we can't see him?"

"Well," said Grandpa, "that reminds me of a story I want to tell you about the six little mice who lived in a piano.

"Six little mice were born in the far corner inside the grand piano in the living room. At breakfast these little mice always tucked their napkins under their chins and ate their stewed felt cereal that their mother had made out of the felt from the piano hammers. If the mice had been well behaved all day, their mother gave them cheese for supper. They used to play tag all around inside the piano, and they sometimes would go skating on the wires.

"Their mother, who had tiny whiskers, was very wise, and as the little mice grew older, they began to ask her questions. Of course they had never been permitted to go outside the piano and so the inside of the piano was the only place they knew.

" 'What is the sky made of, Mother?'

" 'Use your eyes,' she answered. 'Look over your heads. You can see that it is solid mahogany.'

" 'Well, what is the earth like?' they asked her.

" 'Can't you see that for yourselves, too?' she asked them. 'The earth is a flat box affair like a triangle with long wires and wood under our feet and wood everywhere over our heads. Up and down through the world run a great many wires which vibrate and make noises. At one end of these wires are tiny little hammers covered with pieces of felt. These little hammers strike the wires, and that is how the wires make noises called music.'

"It all seemed very wonderful and all six little mice thought, 'What a dear, wise mother we have!' One day as the mice grew older, and wiser, too, they said, 'Mother, what we want to know is what *makes* the hammers strike the wires and make the music?'

" 'Why, the hammers just strike, of course,' said their mother.

" 'Yes, Mother, but *why* do the hammers strike the wires? Who makes them strike?'

"Their mother rolled her eyes up, tweeked her whiskers with her front paw and looked, oh so wise, as she said, 'My mice, you should know that it is the nature of hammers to act that way. That's the way hammers act; they just strike. That's all we know because it's all we can see.'

"But the mice were suspicious and not satisfied. They were thinking hard. 'Isn't there anything beyond this piano in which we live, Mother?' they insisted. You see, they were getting restless. They wanted to know more and to go places.

" 'Can you *see* anything besides this piano?' she asked. 'Of course, there was your grandfather; when he was a very old mouse and not much given to dancing or hunting cheese any more, he ventured outside the piano, and he had wonderful dreams of what he had seen.

" 'In those dreams he saw another world outside this piano where giants walked around on two legs and didn't have any fur on their skins. He sometimes even dreamed of oceans of water with ships sailing on them, and of pretty lights hung up in a dark sky at night. Why, in fact, he used to try to make us believe that the strangest things existed in some fairyland outside our piano box. Poor Grandpa! Of course, we all knew he was getting old, and that he had grown soft in his head. The poor dear was crazy.' Then she said, 'Now run along and be careful not to get hit by a hammer on your little heads, and don't ask any more foolish questions. Be content with what you can see and with what you can touch and hear inside this piano where you were born.'

"But each day the little mice kept getting older, and one of them became very big and bold. He decided one day that he was going to walk over to the edge of the piano and see for himself what he could see. It was at a time when the hammers were striking on the wires and the little mouse's heart went pitapat. But he walked out to the edge of the box and came timidly to the rack where the music is kept. He sniffed and sniffed with his little nose. He just peeked around the corner of a sheet of music. There sat a big man in front of the piano, striking the white ivory keys, and it was this big man who made the hammers strike the wires, to play beautiful music.

"The little mouse was so frightened he ran back into the piano as fast as he could scamper. He told his little brothers and sisters what he had seen of the other world outside their piano house. He told them there was someone big and wonderful who made all the lovely music. They all sat around in a circle and brushed their whiskers back with a grand air, and scratched their tiny ears in a know-it-all way and said, 'Brother, you are just like Grandpa. We don't believe you. It can't possibly be true!'

"Now, really, was the little mouse telling the truth after all?"

THE ADVENTURES OF A SMILE

(*Cheerfulness*)

THE MORNING WAS cool and rainy and gray and the sidewalks were puddled with little looking glasses.

Betty stooped down, grunting a bit in her uncomfortable, bulky raincoat, and pulled on her red boots. The hood slid part way down her head and she pushed it out of her eyes with an angry thrust of her hand.

"Nasty rain, ugly raincoat, clumsy old boots!" She kicked her foot hard against the floor.

Betty's mother came into the hall and smiled. Betty saw the smile as she leaned down to gather up her books from the chair, and she frowned a little as she thought, "Mother can smile because she doesn't have to go out in the rain and spend a whole day in school."

The schoolbooks slipped against the sleeve of Betty's raincoat and went slamming onto the floor. "Oh, these stupid things!" Betty was close to tears as she and her mother knelt to gather up the strewn books, but the mother smiled again as she helped her frowning daughter.

"It's a beautiful morning, Betty dear," she said. "Let's have a smile to start the day."

"Do you call this a beautiful morning? Look at the sloppy walks and the ugly sky. I've got to try to stay dry and go to school and study and stay in at recess, and . . ."

"Betty, God sent the rain this morning to help you. It's melted all of the dirty snow from the lawns and washed the air clean. Everything smells sweet and new like spring. Pretty soon you will be able to jump rope and play jacks and run on the green grass and be shaded from a hot sun by leafy trees. If it weren't for the rain these things wouldn't be. Now let's start the day with an adventure. Lots of people don't know spring is here and they're only going to see mud and rain and gray skies. It's up to you to make them see new buds and tiny blades of grass and hear the birds that have come back to spend the spring and summer with us."

"But, Mother, how can I make them see and hear those things?" asked Betty.

"Smile, dear. It won't be *your* adventure, but the adventure of *your smile*. Maybe you'll never know what happens to that smile, but it will go a long way today if only you're willing to start it on its way. Wear it like sunshine and everyone who sees it will take a part of it and pass it along."

At the door Betty turned and smiled before she went out and called back over her shoulder, "Here's a part of my smile, Mother. Share it, won't you?"

Betty ran down to the main sidewalk where the postman was just turning in. "Good morning, Mr. Tracy, isn't this a lovely new day?" Her smile shone out from under her rain hood and Mr. Tracy couldn't help but smile back.

"Betty, I hadn't thought so until now, but looking at such a bright-eyes as you, I guess maybe it is." His big black slicker rustled on up toward the house and Mr. Tracy was still smiling as he put the mail in the box.

The Rev. Mr. Wheeler unlocked the door of the church study and looked back at the dismal day.

"Hi, Mr. Wheeler, isn't it a nice morning?" Betty grinned as she slid in a muddy spot. "Spring is really wet, but I like it. It smells so nice and the birds are all singing."

The old minister thought about Betty's words and smiled as she went by. "Yes, yes," he murmured to himself. "Spring is making it a nice morning with the help of pretty little smiling faces like Betty's." He closed the door on the dripping weather and hurried to his study to write a sermon about the importance of smiles.

Betty turned the corner and waited for Pete, the school policeman, to help her across. He looked unhappy and chilly. "Got a cold this morning and now all this rain," he said mournfully.

Betty smiled. "Spring is too nice to miss, so don't be sick and have to stay in very long, will you, Pete? I don't know how we could get along without you."

Pete watched her go and shook his head with a smile. "That's a nice girl. Always so bright and happy, she makes a fellow feel better just to see her pretty smile." And he turned to help another group of children across the busy street and grinned at them as they splashed across the puddles.

Betty took off her raincoat and boots in the cloakroom and hurried into the classroom. The teacher turned from writing on the blackboard. "Good morning, children. I see you all managed to stay dry on your way to school. Who had adventures in the rain this morning?"

The teacher looked tired and rather uninterested as each child told of seeing a robin, or getting splashed by a car, or slipping into a puddle.

At last it was Betty's turn. "Well, I guess I'm different. Nothing very important happened to me, but I gave part of my smile to my mother this morning and sent the rest out on an adventure."

Then Betty explained that a smile was like sunshine on a rainy day and that it traveled from face to face. To prove it, she stood very still and smiled at the class and smiled at the teacher and every single one smiled back at her.

—Marlis N. Shaver, in *Juniors*

The Runaway Engine

THE RUNAWAY ENGINE

(Appreciation for older leaders)

"I SHOULD LIKE to make a dash down the track by myself without the engineer," said Big Engine to Little Engine in the roundhouse, where they were staying for the night.

"You see," said Big Engine, "I can pull more cars and go a longer distance than any engine around here, because I am the biggest and the strongest. But I always have to wait for that man they call the engineer, before I can go anywhere."

"Yes," said Little Engine, "but only the engineer knows where the switches are, or how to put on the brakes, or how to read red, yellow, and green lights."

"I don't need any brakes or anyone to read the lights for me," said Big Engine, puffing a slow rhythmic puff puff. "Besides, I have a big whistle, and I can blow all the time to make the other trains get out of my way when I am coming," and Big Engine puffed boastfully, as the fires down in his boiler began to grow hotter and hotter, making more and more steam.

"Well, I always wait for the engineer," said Little Engine. "I think that is the best way."

"Yes, you little engines do," said boastful Big Engine, "but not me. I can take care of myself!" The boiler began to get up more steam as the fires raged and soon the vibration of the steam little by little shook the engine and jarred the throttle open, and swish, 61 dash, choo, choo, down the track wheels spinning, sparks shooting, whistle blowing, steam screeching, away went Big Engine in a wild runaway without the engineer.

"Good-by, 'fraidy cat," said Big Engine to Little Engine. "Tell the engineer, if you ever see him, that I won't need him any more."

Now Big Engine was gathering speed and going faster down the track. He felt so proud of himself as he went roaring by the railroad depot where the surprised people on the platform were waiting for a passenger train.

The man in the switch tower, when he saw Big Engine roaring by, threw up his hands, for he thought he must have lost his reasoning. The gate tender at the crossing did not have time to lower the gate, because he did not expect any train at that time. Big Engine hit an automobile at the crossing and two good people were killed. Still Big Engine kept going faster and faster down the track.

Angry people shouted, "Stop that engine!"

The men in the telegraphic office were sending frantic wires, "Stop the runaway engine. Stop that engine."

By now, when Big Engine saw the damage he had done, he wanted to stop himself, but he didn't know how. There was no engineer to apply the brakes. "I want to stop, I want to stop," he screamed as he rushed along. Ahead he saw a narrow bridge. "I know if I go fast over that bridge," he panted, "I will fall off and go plunging down into the river below and be buried in the deep water." He shuddered at the thought of his terrible end.

But just before he reached the bridge, there was a sharp curve. The engine was going too fast to make the curve, so he ran off the track fell over on his side puffing and panting and blowing.

Soon down the railroad track came the wrecking train and with steel girders they hoisted the engine back onto the track. Then the engineer climbed up into the cab of the engine, opened the throttle very slowly, and guided Big Engine safely back to the roundhouse. He backed him into his stall beside Little Engine for the night.

It was dark now and Big Engine was glad. He was so ashamed of himself that he didn't want Little Engine to see him blush and look disgraced. He was glad it was dark. He wondered what Little Engine would say to him.

62   But Little Engine never said anything unkind; he just said in a

cheery voice, "It's nice, Big Engine, having you back here again."

Big Engine replied, "Thank you, Little Engine, for wanting me back. I also thought it was nice to have my engineer back, too, to guide me and show me the way to get home."

And that was the last time that Big Engine ever started out without the engineer.

THE SIDEWALK LAVENDER PREACHER

(Appreciation for little evidences of beauty in life)

BETTY AND JOHN went to Philadelphia to see the Liberty Bell and Independence Hall where the Declaration of Independence was signed by our early American patriots.

They walked together down an old, narrow street called Chestnut Street, where Benjamin Franklin used to walk. The winter wind was blowing, and Betty and John tipped their heads to sniff the tangy, brisk air, when Betty suddenly stopped her brother John. Her nose was twitching like a bunny rabbit.

"What's that I smell, John?" she demanded.

John wiggled his nose, sniffed, and said, "I just got a whiff of beautiful perfume like flowers blooming somewhere."

They both looked at the hard pavement of the sidewalk and the cement of the street. They knew no flower gardens could grow there, and besides it was winter when flowers did not bloom in the frost and cold.

Like a detective, John followed along the sidewalk the trail of fragrance sniffing and saying, "Where is it coming from?"

Just then Betty heard a voice on the wind say, "Take home lavender, buy sweet lavender."

They both saw the man at the same time. He was an old man on crutches, for he was lame, and he was leaning against the stone building. He was wearing a fur cap and mittens, trying to keep warm. His face was red with the cold wind and weather-beaten. Around his neck, hanging by two strings, was a shallow wooden tray which rested out in front of his chest. This tray was piled with purple-colored flower buds which gave off a sweet fragrance on the December air.

63

The old man smiled at John and Betty, "Take home sweet lavender, sweet lavender," he said. He had little packages of lavender to sell to those who passed by.

John and Betty smelled some of the pretty envelopes of lavender. They did smell so lovely. They gave the man a quarter for three of the little packages. Betty put one in her pocketbook. John put one in his handkerchief pocket, and they said, "We'll take this one home to Mother."

"Do you come here and do this every day?" asked John.

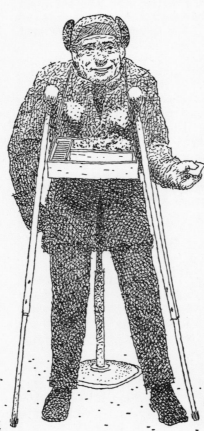

"Yes," said the man, "I have been here nearly every day, except when I have been sick, for almost forty years. I've seen all kinds of people pass by, in all kinds of weather."

"Ooooo, that's an awful long time, isn't it?" said Betty.

You see, Betty and John were really too young to understand how many tens of thousands of packages of lavender, smelling like the sweet perfume of summer gardens, this old man had sent out through the city in all those long years.

"Do you stand here all alone?" asked Betty.

"Well, yes," said the man, shifting his crutch to make it easier under his arm. "You see, my wife is nearly blind, and she can't come with me."

Betty and John walked slowly down the street. They heard auto horns, brakes screeching, traffic officers whistling, and the big buses grinding, but above all the traffic noises, they could hear a gentle voice chanting along the street, "Buy sweet lavender, take home lavender."

64

Just then the newsboys began to shout: "Read all about the big hydrogen bomb blast!"

Still above the shrill voices of the news of bursting bombs, they heard the old man's voice softly trailing along, "Take home the sweet scent of lavender. Buy fragrance."

The noises of the city street mingled into a long, low roar, but as John and Betty moved farther away down the street above it all they could hear like a faint whisper trailing away in the distance, "Take home fragrance, buy sweet lavender."

John and Betty were glad that, like the old man who had never stopped selling and spreading fragrance around through summer and winter all those long years, they, too, were taking home a little whiff of summer fragrance to make others happy in December.

THE CIRCUIT RIDER

(Helping in God's work)

MOLLY STOOD beside her mother in the open doorway of their log cabin and watched her father dismount from his horse. His face looked tired and worn, but as his wife and daughter walked out to greet him, a warm smile lighted his lean face.

"It's good to be home again," he said simply, putting his arms about the girl and her mother.

"It's good to have you home, Stephen," said Elizabeth Clark, helping her husband carry his saddlebags into the small house.

"We're having a delicious supper tonight, Father," said Molly eagerly, her blue eyes shining. "When Mother said she thought you would be home today, we made some cornbread dodgers. We're having them with pork, and honey for sweetening. I went out this morning and picked some wild greens, too, and they're boiling in a kettle in the fireplace right now."

"That all sounds very good to me, Molly," said her father. "The people have had a long, hard winter, so food has been scarce. They gave me what they could, but," he smiled at her, "nothing as good as you have promised."

"Was it a hard trip, Stephen?" asked his wife sympathetically.

65

"Yes, it was, Elizabeth, but I think everyone was glad to see me. Neighbors are so far apart here on the Illinois prairie that they have to provide everything for themselves except religion and news, and it is up to me to provide that."

Molly sat down at her father's knees, listening to him talk. Her father had been gone for almost three months, and she and her mother had missed him very much. He was a traveling preacher, or circuit rider. He rode his horse through the muddy roads from cabin to cabin, preaching, giving out the latest news, marrying young people, saying burial words for the dead, and starting Sunday schools. Sometimes he even had to settle disputes. He stayed for his meals and lodging at the various cabins he visited.

It just did not seem fair that her father should have to be gone so much, thought Molly, a bit rebelliously, as she helped her mother prepare their simple evening meal. Work was hard, for Molly and her mother had to cut their own firewood to burn in the small fireplace that provided the cabin's heat, and they plowed the loose forest earth for their garden. Clothes had to be carried for washing to a little creek about a mile from the house, and the soap used to wash the clothes had been made by Molly and her mother. They raised everything they ate, and spun their own wool for their clothes, even the heavy black suits that the Rev. Mr. Clark wore.

"Are you going to stay home this time, Father?" asked Molly.

Stephen Clark looked at his daughter and then at his wife, who was listening for his answer, too.

"I thought I would wait until tomorrow to tell you," he replied, "but since you have asked—I have to leave again the day after tomorrow."

Molly jumped up from her hardwood bench and ran to her father's side, "Oh, please, Father," she pleaded, "can't you stay at home with us all the time? We need you just as much as those other people do!"

Stephen Clark's face was grave as he gazed down at the small girl whose cinnamon-colored braids touched the shoulders of her faded blue dress. He put a comforting arm around her.

"There's nothing I would like better than to stay at home with you and your mother, Molly, but I'm afraid these people do need me more than you do. They need someone to preach the Word of God to them, and to tell them of Jesus' teachings and his wondrous miracles. It is their faith in God and his word that helps them to bear the rigorous prairie winters and the hardships they must undergo to make a living. They depend on me and I cannot fail them."

"I'm sorry, Father. I'm afraid I sounded very selfish."

Molly's father smiled at her. "You are not selfish, Molly. Actually you and your mother are being very unselfish to carry on alone like this most of the time so that I can help my people. I understand that you would like to have me home with you, and perhaps one of these days things may be as you wish. The people of Grand Detour are planning to erect a church very soon—the first in this part of the country—and one of the reasons I am leaving so soon is so that I can talk to all my friends and try to enlist their help in building the church. When the church is built the people will come to me instead of my having to go to them. When that happens I shall be able to be home with you more often."

Molly smiled at her father and mother, happy to know that they soon would be a real family, but proud, too, of her father, for she realized now what an important part he played in the lives of the people of Illinois. Even though it meant that she and her mother would have a lonely, hard life for a while longer, it was satisfying to know that they were doing their part in carrying on God's work in the world.

—Dorothy Nelson Anstett, in *Juniors*

A BASEBALL FLOP

(Temperance)

SOME SMALL boys were playing baseball after school in a field when a strange man came along who seemed to think that because he was a big, grown-up man he could show little boys how to play baseball.

This man, I am sorry to tell you, had just come from a tavern where he had drunk intoxicating liquor. The alcohol he drank sent its poison through his body though he did not know it. His muscles could not pull together quickly, his eyes were slow to see things, and his lips could not sound his words correctly. Still he swaggered and thought he was the "Cat's pajamas."

He walked up to the plate, took the bat out of Billy's hand, and said, "Hullo there, boyshs. Let ME showsz you boys how to play basheball." Because he was so big and strange, the boys didn't dare to say. "You can't take Billy's bat." They knew that they would have to let this bully have his way, at least for a time.

Jimmy was the pitcher of the team and he thought he would pitch the stranger a good, straight ball to see what he could do with the bat. Jimmy sent a ball right over the plate, but the grown-up man didn't see the ball until after it had passed him, and then he swung his bat at the air with all his might. In fact, he swung it so hard that he could not stand on his feet and fell to the ground.

While the boys watched him, he picked himself up shouting, "Where's the bashe?" and started to run for third base. You see, the alcohol made him think that when he hit the ground, he had hit the ball, when he hadn't hit the ball at all. He ran from third base to the plate again and put his thumbs to his shoulders and crowed, "That wash a home run, boysh."

The boys knew that it wasn't any home run at all and were they disgusted! Even half-grown boys can see through a faker. The boys went into a huddle to find out what to do with this big "buttinski" who was breaking up their game.

The drunken man said, "Here, you let me be the catchsher and show you how to catsch the ball."

"All right," the boys answered and gave him the catcher's glove.

"I'll showsz you some big league baseball," said the staggering catcher, who did not even notice that he was standing in a muddy, greasy place. The rain had made the place where the catcher would stand very slippery. Jimmy pitched a high ball, and when the grown-up man tried to reach for it on his unsteady legs, he went down in the mud with a tail spin, kersplash in mud and goo. He pulled himself slowly up, his hands and face dripping and smeared with mud, and shouted angrily, "I'm going home. You boysh are dumb. You can't learn anything. You don't know how to play basheball."

As he walked away, the boys said, "Boy, are we glad to see him go away! We'll say that he is the dumb one. So stiff and lousy with drink that he couldn't even see the ball coming. I'm glad he's not my father."

"Well," said Jimmy, "he didn't teach us how to play baseball, but he did teach us that if we ever want to be Mickey Mantles, we'll have to leave that poison alcohol alone."

HOW DO YOU SAY YOUR PRAYERS?

(Prayer)

A MAN NAMED John Ruskin discovered that some shepherds in the Alps mountains have a most beautiful way of saying their prayers each still night. If I tell you about them, perhaps you will think of them when you kneel down beside your bed and say your prayers tonight.

Though it seems strange to us to hear of shepherds on mountains as high as the Alps, it does not seem strange to these strong and wise shepherds that they should lead their sheep up the steep trails to soft pastures. They are kind and careful men, who guide their sheep in safety up the dangerous paths to upland fields, where the grass is green and luscious and where even higher up roses and edelweiss bloom through the snow.

You may be sure it is very quiet and lonely, so high on these mountain pastures, where the shepherd stands guarding his flock. In these beautiful fields the air is pure and the silence deep. The flowers, the stars, and the great mountains are friends together. These shepherds, who live out-of-doors so much alone, learn to love God and all his beautiful world. By the tender care of their sheep they remind us of Jesus, the Good Shepherd, who cares for us all.

And when John Ruskin visited these shepherds he discovered their own beautiful way of saying their prayers each still night.

When the sun is setting behind the lofty mountains the snow-covered peaks turn into glistening colors of bright rose, velvet purple, and yellow gold. Slowly the bright colors grow pale and fade as the day is dying. Just then the shepherd who is highest up on the mountain takes his horn from his belt, stands out on a rock, and putting his horn to his lips, blows, with all his strength, a short musical call. It is the music that says, "Glory be to God," and it floats far and wide, borne on the wings of the clear, pure air, down the mountain, into the valley below and across the eternal stillness.

In the next pasture below on the steep mountainside, the nearest shepherd rouses from his reverie as his ears catch the floating notes of the golden music saying, "Glory be to God." He, too, walks across his pasture to the edge of the mountain side looking down the valley, and standing upon a high rock, puts his horn to his lips and repeats the notes of the musical call to prayer which he has just heard coming down to him from above. "Glory be to God," he blows on his horn, sending the music forth upon the mountain air and letting it float downward slowly to the nearest shepherd in the pasture below.

In the rosy twilight and through the gathering nightfall each shepherd, who hears the call to prayer from afar, repeats the music upon his own horn until, says John Ruskin, all the shepherds across a hundred miles of mountains have heard and answered the call, "Glory be to God."

So I like to think that when the great sun sets in the west, turning the sky to red and gold, and the shadows creep up toward the night, and Mother calls us to go to bed, that we too hear a call from the Great Shepherd who is highest up on the mountain, and we fall on our knees to give thanks and glory to God, our Maker and kind heavenly Father.

PATIENCE AND THE PADLOCK

(A historical incident to inspire church loyalty)

PATIENCE JOSLIN was a child who grew up in a Puritan home. Today we do not name our babies the way the Pilgrims and Puritans did. Patience, you see, was a very beautiful, but a very quaint name, too. And Patience Joslin had quaint ways of doing things, as, for instance, the time when she got the heavy iron padlock off the church door. It had taken several men to put the padlock on, because it was so big and heavy. But Patience got it off all by herself. And this was the way it happened.

Many, many years ago, sometime after the Pilgrims and the Puritans came in their boats to Massachusetts Bay Colony, their children, as they grew up, moved farther into the forest and built a town they called Leominster. They named it after an old town in the mother country of England. After a while, of course, they built a church of logs—a log-cabin church. And then, one day in the summer, when it was very dry, the log-cabin church caught fire and burned to the ground.

There were more people in the town now, and so they built a

little white church in place of their old log-cabin church. The church was very small, but everyone expected that it would grow and that they could someday have a bigger church. But, for some strange reason, the church did not grow.

Many people in the town grew tired of going to church. They forgot to honor and worship God. They grew weary of giving money to keep the church doors open. Soon the church was too small and poor to have a pastor any longer, and, at last, there were only six

71

members left in the congregation of the little church in Leominster.

One night the six people called a meeting to decide what they could do.

"Let us close the church doors and put a padlock on the door," said one man.

The other men said, "It is no use. We can't keep the church open any longer. We have no minister; we have no money, and people do not come. Yes, let's padlock the church."

When they took a vote, the five men voted to close the church and put a heavy padlock on the church door.

But the sixth person, Patience Joslin, stood up and pleaded, "No, no! You mustn't close the doors of the house of prayer. This is the house of God, and it must be kept open on the Sabbath Day."

But the men only looked at each other and said, "Who is she? She is only a woman in the town. We know what is best to do. Pay no attention to Patience Joslin." So they put a big padlock on the front of the church door and turned the heavy iron key, to let everyone know that the church was closed and would be used no more.

But they had not counted on the power of Patience Joslin, who loved the church, and who had faith that God would help her to keep open his house of prayer, even in this town where people had forgotten God. Each Sunday morning, all through the long winter, Patience Joslin knelt in prayer in the snow before the padlocked church door, asking God to help her open his church. Every prayer-meeting night she again knelt before the church door. As the people of the town passed by they saw her praying there.

Little by little, they began to feel ashamed of themselves to see this lone woman praying outside because she could not get into the church. Besides they missed the ringing of the church bell with its holy call, sounding on the crisp morning air. Some of them began to wish they could go to church once more and sing the hymns.

Week after week, Patience Joslin kept her vigil on her knees before the padlocked church door. When June came, and the daisies and buttercups swayed before the wind like a yellow sea in the meadows, the village folk called a meeting and voted to reopen the church. On the next Sabbath the people were so happy to be back in church again! They all gave money so they could have a pastor, and, soon, so many people came that they had to build still another new church to hold the crowds. Today this church has nearly a thousand members. Its doors are wide open nearly every day of the week, with happy voices coming from within, from boys and girls and men and women.

And, best of all, they have not forgotten the woman to whose prayers they owe this church—Patience Joslin. For, in the lobby of this house of worship, where all may see it who come and go, hangs the picture, painted by a famous New York artist, of Patience Joslin in her Puritan hat and simple dress, kneeling in the snow in front of the iron-padlocked door of the church. As the people see her picture of faith and prayer, they, too, resolve to love the house of God more dearly and to persevere in what they know to be right, just like Patience Joslin.

SOFT WORDS TURN AWAY WRATH

(Control of temper)

IN A LITTLE Vermont town the selectmen one day put up a strange-looking sign. It said:

"By order of the Selectmen, cows grazing by the roadside or riding bicycles on the sidewalk is hereby forbidden."

Of course the selectmen never meant that cows were not to be allowed to ride bicycles on the sidewalk. They were thinking only of boys and girls, and that is quite a different thing.

Still, it is a temptation to boys and girls to ride their bicycles on a smooth sidewalk, and in spite of rules, they sometimes do.

In fact, one day as I sat by my window in that little Vermont town, I saw a boy on a new bicycle come riding down the sidewalk so swiftly that he bumped right into a man and almost knocked him down. Now the man became terribly angry and he shouted out in rage. He was angry because he had been bumped and smeared with dust, and also because he knew that the boy was breaking the law.

With a quick firm jerk, the angry man seized the handle bars of the bicycle, and let his temper fly at the boy. "I'll have you arrested!" he shouted. "The judge will fix you! I'll teach you, young fellow, not to ride bicycles on the sidewalk and break the law!"

Of course the boy was in the wrong, and he should have admitted it at once. But like most boys he lost his temper, too, and became very, very angry. "Oh, no, you won't!" he shouted right back. "You take your hands off my bicycle!"

73

Then the man grew even more angry than before. With a new threat in his angry voice, he yanked the bicycle out of the boy's grip and cried, "I'll see that this bicycle is taken away from you, I will! I'll fix it so that you'll lose your bicycle. You'll never ride this again!"

That threat of losing his beautiful new bicycle brought the boy to his senses. He loved his bicycle, for he had worked hard to earn the money to buy it, and he had had to save up his money for a long, long time.

The boy jumped right down off his high horse of temper and sauciness. Then he said in a very mild and manly voice, "Say, mister, I'm very sorry. You're right and I am wrong."

The angry man was quite surprised to hear the boy talk like that. "Didn't you know that you were breaking the law?" he said in not-quite-so-angry a voice.

"Yes," admitted the boy, "but I just forgot. I really didn't mean to disobey, and I'm very sorry I hit you, sir."

The man let go one hand from the boy's bicycle. "Well, are you going to stop this riding on the sidewalk?" he demanded in a still-less-angry voice.

"Yes, sir, and I promise you that I'll be very careful and not do it ever again."

The man let go his other hand off the bicycle. This time he put his hand on the boy's shoulder.

"Now you're talking," the man said in a voice-that-was-not-angry-at-all. "Why, I wouldn't think of taking a new bicycle away from a fine lad like you, and of course I wouldn't think of taking you up before the judge either. I just forgot myself for a moment and lost my temper. Now let's shake hands like good friends, and mind you keep off the sidewalk after this."

The man went sauntering down the street, brushing the dust from his clothes, and the boy jumped merrily on his new bike and was gone in a flash. The tempest was over.

Perhaps the man had suddenly remembered how it was when he was a boy, or perhaps both the man and boy had remembered a Bible verse they had learned in Sunday church school, "A soft answer turns away wrath, but a harsh word stirs up anger."

74

A GREAT EXPLORER PRAYS

ALL TRULY GREAT men have always been friends of God who trusted him and put their faith in him. They were men who knew that God helped them up the hard pathways of their lives.

I want to tell you about one such great man named Roald Amundsen. Roald was born in Norway. When he was a young boy, he loved to think of himself growing up to be an explorer. This brave, bold career excited him, though it is a rare ambition. Reading of the lives of great explorers sparked within him the idea of going to places where no man before had ever set foot.

At the age of eight years, when other boys were playing simple games, Roald was hardening his body and climbing dangerous hills the better to meet the challenge he knew he wanted to face in his future.

When he was a boy, most of the world had been traveled over and explored except the far North Pole and the South Pole, where desolate wastes of snow and ice and treacherous seas abound. When Roald was very young, he would often ask, "Mother, why did God make such lonely isolated outposts in the world while so many other things are so beautiful?" His mother, wise peasant women that she was, would rap him on his head sharply with her thimble and tell him not to question the ways of God.

"Fetch some firewood," she said.

His mother wanted him to become a doctor, but Roald held fast to his dreams of exploring and finding both the North Pole and the South Pole. Why, he did not know, but his ambition stayed with him all his life.

When he was only sixteen, he set forth. He became a cabin boy on a ship that was exploring the vast and dangerous seas about the South Pole. On the ship he was so smart he was soon promoted to second mate. Because he had read so many books, he knew how to loose the endangered ship from the ice floes in which it had become frozen.

Later on, with almost no money, but with willing and enthusiastic shipmates, he purchased for himself a broken-down ship and sailed into the white and gray unknown seas of the North. He hoped to reach the North Pole. He never did, but he was the first man to find the Northwest Passage. This was a way by sea from the Atlantic Ocean to the Pacific Ocean. He entered the Arctic by way of Greenland, sailed ever north and emerged off the coast of Alaska.

Not long thereafter, Commodore Peary of the United States discovered the North Pole, and Roald's dream, one half of it, was shattered. But he had still more dreams and later he was the first man ever to sail over the North Pole in an airship. While looking down at the fierce and barren land of ice and snow, he spoke a prayer to God and dropped the flags of several nations.

On December 14, 1911, Roald Amundsen, accompanied by four men and a team of dog sleds, dashed to the South Pole. There again, remembering God his great Friend, he knelt in the snow as the earth whirled about and beneath him at the southernmost tip of God's world. He thanked God for his triumph and humbly prayed for deliverance in getting back to his base.

On the way back, his party came across the frozen bodies of Robert Scott, a brave British explorer, and his team, which had been racing Amundsen to the South Pole. They were all dead of hunger and cold. Again Amundsen thoughtfully turned to God under the cold, twinkling stars of the Far Below, and prayed for strength to reach home. On his return, he received honors from the whole world.

When Amundsen died he did so in the noblest tradition of men who go down to the seas or explore the unknown places of the earth. He went out on a mercy mission to save an Italian explorer, Nobile, who had crashed at the North Pole. Oddly, Amundsen and the explorer, one Umberto Nobile, had never really liked each other. But when the radio flashed that Nobile was stranded on the ice and in great danger, Amundsen took off to rescue him. This was his last flight. He was never heard from again. His body was never found.

But all throughout his life, Roald Amundsen maintained a firm belief in God and in his drive to chart the uncharted areas of the world. As he said before he was lost forever from this earth, "Above and beyond skill and determination, there is a faith that can move mountains and reach the distant shores. Through storms and terror, I always was enabled to find a peaceful haven because of my prayer to the One above. It is a thing that confounds all scientists."

HOW ONE MAN SAVED A CHURCH

(*Church loyalty*)

ABOUT ONE HUNDRED years ago, a little Baptist church was started at the corner of Erie and Howe Streets, in the city of Cleveland, Ohio. The congregation had purchased a church building from another denomination, but to do so they had to go deeply in debt.

For nine years the little congregation struggled along. But then, worn out from trying to pay off their debt, and discouraged because so many people did not seem to care enough to help, the little congregation decided to close their church. The clerk was instructed to grant letters of dismission to any and all who wished to take their membership elsewhere. Then the doors of the little church were locked. That was in July, 1860.

But there was one member of that little church who refused to quit. Like Nehemiah in the Bible, he had nobody else to consult, so he consulted himself. In that way he secured unanimous consent to hold a one-man prayer meeting on the steps every Wednesday.

Of course this one man missed the warm fellowship he had enjoyed when the church was open, and many people came together to worship. But he soon learned to depend more and more upon having fellowship with God, his heavenly Father.

Now genuine prayer always brings its reward. At first, this church-steps worshiper winged his prayers upward for divine refreshing. Then he began to give legs to his prayers, to carry them out into the neighborhood. Before long, he discovered another church member who was willing to join him on the church steps every Wednesday evening. The two men found two more. The four found another four, and the eight soon grew to sixteen.

Then autumn arrived. The nights were too chilly for church-step meetings. Should the little band stop holding services until warmer weather? No, they needed to worship God even when it was cold, and they did love their fellowship together. Should they go to some home where they might find warmth and welcome? No, this would take the people away from their church with all its sacred memories. So, there was only one thing to do: the little group decided to ask the trustees to reopen the church. And when they saw how earnest the people were, the trustees gladly consented to open the doors again.

Now the church-steppers did not doze off as soon as they were admitted to a comfortable room. The rekindled fires of enthusiasm burned brightly, and soon the building was filled with eager people who decided that the time had come for them to call a pastor. The church property was deeded to one of the deacons, who agreed to pay off the debt. Then he leased the building back to the church.

Another one of the deacons in that old Erie Street church was an excellent Bible teacher. From his Bible class came many of the future leaders of the church.

One Sunday a fourteen-year-old boy came into Deacon Sked's class. Some people in the church said that you could not expect much from this boy, because he was too impractical. But he kept on coming to the class, and the next year he joined the church. At that time, he was earning only $4.50 a week and was boarding himself, but he always gave a part of his earnings to the church. The boy, soon grown to become a man, was a member of that church for seventy-two years, until long after the name of John D. Rockefeller became famous.

After a few years, the church moved to the corner of Euclid Avenue and Huntington (now Eighteenth Street). In 1868, the church was known as the Second Baptist Church, but in 1877, it chose the more meaningful name of Euclid Avenue Baptist Church. Out of that little one-man congregation grew a great church numbering at one time over two thousand members.

The church was a missionary church. It established several mission churches, a German Baptist Church, and the Baptist Home for Old People. It carried on street preaching, meetings for newsboys, a day nursery for children of mothers who had to work, classes and schools for Italians, Bulgarians, Hungarians, and other foreign-born Clevelanders. Several young men from the church became ministers, and four young women were sent as missionaries to India and China.

Perhaps you would like to know the name of this one man who had saved what became such an important Baptist church. That would be interesting to know, but his name has not been preserved in any of the records. Just as we have the Tomb of the Unknown Soldier in Washington, who represents every person who has given his life for his country, so here we have the church steps of this unknown worshiper who, by his steadfast devotion to God and his church, may represent you and me, if only we will be as loyal.

—Asa Zadel Hall

78

THE RAIN IS GOD'S GIFT

(Appreciation of God's unrecognized gifts)

"OH, SHUCKS," pouted Jim, "now the rain is spoiling our fun."

"It *would* have to rain," joined in Marion, "just when we wanted a day of sunshine for our party."

Jim and Marion were looking out the window from the city apartment house where they lived.

"What a mean, hateful old thing the rain is!" Marion said, turning her wrath on the weather.

"Makes me boiling mad," added Jim, clenching his fists for emphasis.

Just then Jim's mother came up behind the children and looked over their shoulders through the window at the gently falling spring shower.

"Why, there's that new girl standing in her doorway across the street. Look at her, Jim and Marion."

"What on earth is she doing there?" asked Marion. "Doesn't she know that she will get wet without an umbrella? The rain is blowing into the doorway."

"Well, you look again and see if you can find out why she is standing there and what she is doing.

To me she looks very happy right now," pointed out Mother.

Sure enough, Jim could see that his mother was right. The girl had a wondrously bright smile all over her face. The soft rain was falling on her upturned face and running down her forehead, eyes, and cheeks.

79

"Why does she have her face turned up to the rain, getting it all wet?" asked Marion in amazement. "She acts as if it were great fun feeling the raindrops on her cheeks and forehead and all over her face."

"And she is holding out her hands to get them wet, too," Jim went on. "And did you ever see anyone look so thrilled?"

"You are right about her," their mother spoke tenderly. "Our new neighbor is grateful to have the sensation of raindrops on her skin. It is one of her special joys in life. There are so many things she misses, so many sights and colors, that she has learned to be grateful for small touches, even of the spring rain."

Jim and Marion stood at the window staring across the street in silence a long time.

Then Marion asked, "Mother, she is young and pretty, isn't she, but is she really blind?"

"Yes," said her mother, "she is blind and cannot see."

"And is it always as dark as night to her?" asked Jim.

"It is always darkness to her," said the mother.

The children looked through the window at the girl again as she stood there in the rain. This time her face seemed a prayer of thanks to God that he had sent the spring showers to brush her cheek, to gently pat her face, and to make music for her ears to hear.

When Jim and Marion started for school they lifted their heads toward the sky just to feel what it was like to have the wonderfully friendly, soft rain on their faces. In fact, they crossed the street and said to the new girl in the neighborhood, "Would you like to walk to school with us?"

When she said a gleeful, "Yes," Marion exclaimed, "Oh, I just love the rain, don't you?"

And the new girl smiled as Marion took her arm and said, "Oh, the rain is so friendly! I love its soft kisses, its gentle pats, and even its warm stings."

"You bet," said Jim, who but a half hour ago had been grumbling and growling like an old grumpy bear about the hateful rain. "You bet!" Taking a look again at the girl's blind eyes, "I think the rain is beautiful, too!"

80

THE COURTESY OF A KIND HEART

(A true story to encourage good manners*)

"I HATE BEING polite," said John. "I'm tired of saying, 'If you please,' 'Excuse me,' and 'I beg your pardon.'"

I'm afraid John's sister Dot sometimes felt the same way, too. It was so easy to be rude and so hard to be polite all the time.

"But didn't you know," said Mother, "that it really is kingly to be polite, and regal to show courtesy? Some of our most polite friends," she added, "belong to the royal family of Great Britain." Then she told John and Dot this story.

One day the President of our country, Woodrow Wilson, and his wife, Mrs. Wilson, were invited to Buckingham Palace in London to a banquet being given by King George and the Queen of Great Britain.

It was called a golden banquet because the candlesticks were gold and the dinner was served on golden plates. The goblets that stood beside the plates were gold and there were golden ornaments about the palace banquet room. The servants who served the dinner wore uniforms of crimson red. They had white wigs on their heads and they were dressed in knee breeches, with great golden buckles on their shoes.

To honor the guests from our country, the King and Queen of England asked soldiers from the Tower of London to attend the banquet as guards. These were called yeomen of the guard. They wore tall, black beaver hats with straps under their chins, red coats with gold braid and buttons, and they carried shining spears. These soldiers stood, a few feet apart, against the walls all around the huge banquet hall. They stood without moving a muscle, each like a statue, heads held high, eyes forward, feet together.

Suddenly the President's wife saw coming into the banquet hall a strange-looking man wearing a very high hat and a pink coat with white breeches and shiny shoes. In his hand he was carrying a slender golden wand. She watched to see what this officer in the pink coat would do. She saw him march around the room slowly, stopping in front of each one of these statuelike soldiers. Every time he stopped in front of a soldier, he touched the toes of the soldier's boots with the

---

* This story was suggested by Mrs. Woodrow Wilson's article, which appeared in *The Saturday Evening Post*, the second week of January, 1939.

end of his golden wand and then passed on to do the same to the next soldier.

This was such a strange act that the first lady of our land turned to the king, who was sitting next to her at the banquet table, and asked, "Please, Your Majesty, may I ask why this officer in the pink coat touches all the toes of the boots of all the soldiers who are standing around the walls in this banquet hall?"

The king smiled and said, "I am glad to tell you about this very ancient custom which is still observed. It is really the story of the courtesy of a very kind heart. You see, many hundreds of years ago, there was a banquet held in this same hall and, for the first time, guards from the Tower of London were invited to attend as a guard of honor, and they stood about the hall at attention, just as they are standing here tonight. On that occasion the chief officer of the Tower of London suddenly walked into the banquet hall to inspect his men. He wanted to see if they were all standing up perfectly straight in their military postures, without moving a muscle.

"As he came in he found one of his soldiers who had grown so tired that he had relaxed and had put one foot out in front of the other. This was not proper. The chief officer touched the toe of the tired officer with his golden wand. Suddenly he saw the blood rush to the face of the soldier. His crimson cheeks betrayed his humiliation in having been singled out by his chief officer from all the rest for correction. He was embarrassed before his king.

"Then the chief officer felt very sorry for what he had done to this soldier and wondered what he could do to show that he did not mean to hurt him. Very quickly he thought that if he should march around the hall and touch every soldier on the toe of his boot with his golden wand, it would then look as if this were just a part of the ceremony and the regular thing to do. So, this kind officer, who was too courteous to want one of his men to blush before his king, and too kind to hurt the feelings of even one of his brave soldiers, slowly walked about the hall, touching the toe of every soldier's boot with his golden wand.

"Then," said the king, smiling at Mrs. Wilson, "since that day whenever a banquet is held in this palace, and guards from the Tower of London are brought here as a guard of honor, this same ceremony is still carried out—the ceremony of the golden wand touching the boot of every soldier."

82   The President's wife smiled at the king and at the queen and said,

"What a beautiful memorial to a kind heart! Wherever I go, I shall
do my part to tell the story of this officer's courtesy."

"Well, if our President's wife thought it was nice to be so polite,
I do, too," said Dot.

"And if an officer in the Tower of London is as polite as that,"
said John, "I intend to try, too."

83

ROCKET IS A red-brown Irish setter who belongs to Jim, and they are wonderful pals. It is always together they go, these pals, Jim and Rocket, boy and dog, running across the fields, leaping fences and stone walls, vaulting the ditches, playing tag, or just walking slowly to school. Rocket always looks so sad, hanging his head way down, when he is not allowed to go into the school with Jim.

Jim says to him, "Rocket, what could you do with subtraction or division of fractions? Nouns and verbs are not for dogs, Rocket. So now please go home." And with tail down, Rocket drags himself home, so disappointed.

But on the playground, it is always boy and dog, Jim and Rocket; and it is hard to say who has the more fun, for Rocket plays till he lies down on the ground with his red tongue sticking out, panting for breath, as if to say, "Jim, I'm completely winded."

When Jim goes to the store for his mother, Rocket bounds out of the house, streaks across the lawn and catches up with his master, walking at Jim's heels or weaving leaping circles of joy around his young master, and now and then jumping up to kiss him on the hand or cheek.

Why, Rocket even follows his young master to church and Sunday school. Each Sunday just as the church bells are ringing, "Come to church, come to church," Rocket slips out of the house, somehow, though they try to lock all the doors. Rocket seems to know that this is a different day, for he follows closely beside his master, walking along as solemn as a judge.

But when Jim says, at the church doors, in a low, commanding voice, "Rocket, please go home," he simply walks over to the other side of the street, looking very much hurt, holding his nose up in the air. He waits there, if you please, until the morning worship service is over and Jim comes out.

One bright Sunday morning Rocket did get into the church. Quick as a flash he slid through the front entrance, between the legs of the ushers who were standing there. He walked up the front aisle right during the sermon. He carefully sniffed each pew. Finally he went

84

into one of the empty pews in the middle of the church and there Rocket lay down on the floor with his face resting on his paws, trying to look very pious.

Rocket's sudden presence on the floor of the pew, however, raised a great commotion among the ushers and deacons who began frowning, pointing across the aisles and motioning for someone to take that dog out. Marching down the aisle came two of the ushers trying to collar the dog. They made more disturbance, I'm sure, than quiet Rocket just lying there would ever make.

The pastor, who had a dog of his own, held up his hand and stopped the ushers. With a smile he said, "Let the dog listen to the sermon. It will do him no harm, and if he does go to sleep he will do no worse than some members of my congregation!" And then the minister added with a merry twinkle in his eyes, "If I could only get some of you as excited about getting somebody *into* church as you are trying to throw a harmless dog *out* of the church, what a happy man I would be!"

So Rocket stayed securely in his place through the service, though he felt very sad and lonely in the empty pew. He slunk away home when he saw the people going out.

At the back of the church, after the service was over, the minister and the ushers and deacons were talking about Rocket.

"In what a businesslike way that dog came down the aisle and marched to that empty pew! What do you suppose possessed the dog and made him come to church? He never did this before," said the puzzled pastor.

"I think I have the answer to your question, pastor," said one of the deacons. "You see, I live next door to Jim, and I know how impossible it is to separate Rocket from his master. That dog goes everywhere with Jim. Jim went to the hospital last Tuesday for an operation, and Rocket has been a lonely, homesick, broken-hearted pup all week, going to the school, the store, and the playground, everywhere searching in vain for Jim. He could not find him anywhere. Jim, you know, always comes to church. He wears one of those pins for perfect attendance at Sunday church school. I imagine that when Sunday came and Rocket heard the church bells ringing, he thought he would be sure to find his master at church. So he came in here, sniffing until he smelled out Jim's pew and waited for him there."

"What a smart dog to expect to find his master at the church," said the minister. "And I say, too, what a grand boy is Jim, for when his dog missed him the dog knew where he could look for him to be—in church on Sunday!"

Then the pastor cast a sharp eye on the deacons and ushers and a few members of the congregation who were still standing around. "I wonder how many of you," he said with a roguish smile, "have a dog who would look for you in church, if he missed you on Sunday?"

BEWARE OF THE JIFFIES

(The evils of procrastination)

"YOU MUST always beware of the jiffies," said Mother to Patsy, as Patsy was rushing off late to school.

"What do you mean?" said Patsy.

"Oh, you are always saying, 'Just in a jiffy,'" said Mother. "When you come back, I want to tell you more about the jiffies."

That night after school Patsy said, "Who are the people called 'jiffies' and where do they live?"

"Oh, the jiffies," said her mother. "They have been around a long time. I used to hear your grandfather speak of them. Our family has never liked them. They'll hang around all day long and never go home."

"Are they a big family?" asked Patsy.

"Oh, yes, they have lots of relatives, aunts, uncles, cousins, and everything. There is Just-in-a-Jiffy, he's the worst one. Then In-a-Sec, he is another. Then Coming-soon is one of the cousins, and Don't-rush-me is an uncle, and Time-enough is one of the aunts."

"Well, where do they live and what do they look like? Are they elves?" persisted Patsy.

"Not exactly elves, just jiffies," said her mother. "They are a teeny, weeny folk who live in teeny, weeny houses on Slow Poke Street in Tardytown. They are very skinny and thin, because they are always late to have luncheon. If you ring the doorbell at a jiffy's house, he never rushes downstairs to open the door, but yawns and yawns and yawns and scratches his head and says, 'Just in a jiffy.' They have something sticky on their feet and glue on the patches of their pants. When they walk their feet stick, and when they sit down it takes

86

them a long time to get up. If they ever get on you, the jiffies stick like birds."

"I don't want any jiffies on me," said Patsy in disgust.

"I'm glad to hear that," said Mother, "but yesterday I noticed Just-in-a-Jiffy spent most of the day with you."

"He did?" said Patsy in amazement, "I never saw him!"

"Perhaps you didn't, but I certainly heard him around," said Mother. "When I asked you to bring me a bar of soap from the closet, you said, 'Just in a jiffy.' All day long I heard you call the name of that shrimp of an imp."

"I didn't know that," protested Patsy, surprised to know what she had said and done.

"Oh, that little Just-in-a-jiffy is a contemptible fellow," said Mother. "When his own mother calls him in from play, he pretends to be deaf. He says, 'I didn't hear you, Mother.' When she comes after him with a tiny green switch, he tries to look hurt and says, 'I didn't hear you calling me, but I was coming anyway, just in a jiffy.' He likes to hear his own name repeated."

"I don't want anything to do with the jiffies any more," declared Patsy.

"You had better beware of them," said her mother.

"But how can I tell one when I see one?" said Patsy.

"Well," said her mother, "you can always tell a jiffy, because he has three hands, a right hand, a left hand, and a little behind hand. That's how you can tell a jiffy, by his little behind hand."

THE LITTLE IMPS

(Impossible, impatient, impolite, impudent, self-important, impenitent)

"I DON'T BELIEVE any more in fairies and brownies, and I don't believe in elves and imps, either," said Mary in a firm voice, trying to show her father that now she was a big grown-up girl.

"Well, you are right, Mary," answered her father, "yet, I believe that there are still plenty of little Imps around and they are causing a lot of trouble."

"Do you believe in Imps, Daddy?"

Her father's words made Mary's eyes pop in surprise.

"Daddy believes in Imps," she said to herself in a low whisper.

"Yes, some of the worst Imps go to your school. But there are a number of them who live in our house, too."

By now Mary was so confused that she asked, "What do you mean, Daddy?"

"Come over here by my desk," her father motioned. "Imps," he said, "are very tiny and hard to see." He picked up a pencil from his desk. "The Imps are so small they can sit astride a pencil. In fact, they like to slide down your pencil when you are working in school on a hard arithmetic problem. A bad little Imp slides down your pencil looking straight up at you with saucy eyes and shouting, '*IMP*ossible, *IMP*ossible, *IMP*ossible. You can't do it. You can't do it. It's *IMP*ossible.'" Then with a smile her dad said, "I hope you box his ears so soundly that he will scamper away and never dare to come near your pencil again."

"But you said some Imps are in our house, Daddy. I never saw any here."

"Oh, haven't you?" answered Dad. "Well, let me tell you. I heard one last night when you were getting undressed. He probably crawled through the keyhole in your door. For when you couldn't untie the hard knot in your shoestring, I heard you lose your temper. I knew that *IMP*atient—yes, that bad *IMP*atient—was leering and laughing at you from the toe of your shoe."

Mary was now beginning to catch on. She blushed and asked, "Do we have any other Imps around our house?"

"Oh yes, *IMP*olite likes to hang around and make trouble. When you forget to say 'Thank you' or 'Please may I,' I know that *IMP*olite is sitting there on the rim of your ear whispering, 'Oh, don't bother to say "Thank you" and don't bother to say "Please." I never do. Just be *IMP*olite like me.'"

"I just wish he'd lose his balance and fall like Humpty Dumpty, so he could never be put together again."

"Actually," her father continued, "*IMP*olite has a twin brother whose name is *IMP*udent. Somehow he climbs up on the lips and sits on the corners of the mouth. When you are sulky and talk back to your mother or say when you are asked to do an errand, 'I won't go there now,' of course, it's that mean old *IMP*udent who gets on the tip of your tongue. If you let *IMP*olite and *IMP*udent stay around you very much, they will keep you from being liked by other people, and they will keep you from making friends."

"Well, I hate those Imps anyway," said Mary, who did try hard to be kind and polite.

"I think I have seen an Imp, too," said Mary, who now began to believe in the kind of Imps her father was talking about. "Well," she said, "I think my brother John is very self-*IMP*ortant just because he has a new bicycle. He's so self-*IMP*ortant that he won't let me ride on it ever. Wait and see if I don't pay him back, the old meanie."

"You may be right, Mary. Probably John has let self-*IMP*ortant creep up on him. But when you said you'd pay him back, that was another Imp. You were *IMP*enitent, hard and cold and unforgiving. *IMP*enitent takes all tenderness and forgiveness out of our hearts. But when I hear a boy or girl say, 'I'm sorry, I forgive you, will you forgive me?' then I know they have driven *IMP*enitent out of their hearts. Then I know they have driven the whole gang of *IMP*s— *IMP*ossible, *IMP*atient, *IMP*olite, *IMP*udent, self-*IMP*ortant, and *IMP*enitent out of their hearts and lives."

Mary was very thoughtful for a long time. Then she lifted her head and looking at her father said, "Dad, will you come and look into my room after I get into bed tonight?"

After Mary was snugly tucked in bed that night, her father looked into her bedroom. There he saw a sign stuck on the mirror over her bureau. He walked over and this is what he read, "No Imps Allowed on These Premises."

JERRY FINDS HIS NEIGHBORS

(Neighborliness)

JERRY BRITTON was lonesome. It hadn't been a very happy winter so far. His father was not well, and Jerry missed doing all the things they used to do together. Then they had had to move out West where there was not a neighbor for miles around. Jerry missed his friends at school. They always went sledding or skating down on the pond after school.

Jerry went to school on the bus every day. It was not too bad, riding over the long miles to school. Still, it was not easy to get acquainted with the other fellows. They already had little groups of their own to pal around with. Ben Turner seemed like a nice enough boy. But what was the use of even trying to know him better, when Ben and his family lived nearly ten miles away?

Then winter settled down in earnest, and one Friday morning when Jerry woke, the world was white with snow.

"Oh, boy!" Jerry exclaimed in delight. "This looks more like home, doesn't it, Mother?"

But his mother's eyes were troubled. "This must be one of those storms we've read about," she said anxiously. "They don't occur very often, and I was hoping we wouldn't have one of them—our first winter."

"I wonder if the school bus will run today?" Jerry asked, his voice high in excitement. "I think I'll dash down the road to see."

"Do be careful, son," his mother warned him. "If it keeps on snowing at this rate, nothing can get through. Why, we might even be snowbound for days!"

Mrs. Britton began to worry about her nearly empty pantry shelves. She always did her marketing on Saturdays. Of course, there would be enough canned goods for a while, but her sick husband needed milk and eggs and other fresh foods. And what about the wood supply? The pile in the back of the house was already covered.

Jerry did not worry as he ran out into the driving storm. But after a few minutes he realized that perhaps it was not going to be fun after all.

"I must be nearly to the road now," Jerry said to himself. But then as he turned back, he realized he could not see his house. He found himself sinking deep into drifts every time he tried to take a step. He wondered if he ever would get back to the house.

Then he called, "Yoo hoo!" with all the strength he could muster. But no one answered. He didn't know how long he floundered there in the snow. It seemed like hours. But suddenly he heard a motor chug, chug, chugging along very slowly, and the sound came nearer and nearer.

"Yoo hoo!" Jerry called again.

"Yoo hoo yourself!" came a faint answer above the motor's steady hum.

Then in a few minutes Jerry made out the outline of a giant snowplow, pushing and nosing its way along like some great monster. "Hi! Who's there?" someone called from the cab.

"It's Jerry Britton," he managed to shout. "And I can't find my way back home!"

"Sit tight!" the voice called reassuringly. "Everything's going to be okay!"

The snowplow lunged to a stop and suddenly Ben Turner leaped out, followed by his father. Together they helped Jerry into the cab. Mr. Turner took off his heavy gloves and rubbed the boy's cold hands until they tingled with comforting warmth again.

"But how did you know—" Jerry began, between teeth that still chattered from fright and cold.

"We were worried about you folks," Mr. Turner explained. "So Ben and I got out the old snowplow and started over. "It's never failed us yet, so we knew it wouldn't this time."

"Mom loaded us up with supplies, too," Ben put in eagerly. "She was afraid your mother might run out of food. We don't have storms like this often, but when we do, look out! They're likely to last awhile."

"It's sure lucky for me you happened along," Jerry said. "I was lost all right."

Jerry's parents were so happy and relieved when their son and the Turners stamped in.

"What wonderful neighbors you are!" Mrs. Britton said gratefully.

"And we thought we didn't have any neighbors just because everybody lives so far from everybody else!" Jerry added.

"Being neighborly isn't really a matter of miles, or distance, I guess," Mr. Britton reflected. "It's a way of living—of caring for other folks and sharing with them, too."

Jerry and Ben looked at each other and grinned—two big, happy grins that seemed to say, "What pals we're going to be!"

There would never be a doubt in Jerry's mind again—there are neighbors everywhere!

—Adapted from a story
by Mary Peacock, in *Juniors*.

(Kindness)

ONCE THERE WAS a beautiful queen who lived in a kingdom far across the sea. She was as good and kind and wise as she was beautiful. But also she was not as happy as she wanted to be—and this is the reason for her being so sad.

The lords and ladies of her court were very jealous of each other; they tried to gain favor in the eyes of the queen each for himself. They constantly came to her with unkind stories and gossip about the other courtiers. By this, they tried to lower them in the queen's eyes and thus gain a more favored place for themselves with the queen.

All this bickering and gossip made the queen very unhappy. She wondered what she might do to make her court a happy place. Finally, she called together the wise men of her kingdom to ask their advice on how to deal with the problem which made her so sad. The wise men made many suggestions; some even wanted imprisonment as the punishment of anyone caught bearing tales or gossiping about another lord or lady of the queen's court.

After much discussion one old man said: "Oh, Queen, your courtiers are like naughty children and they should be treated as such."

After listening to his plan, the queen sent out heralds to summon all the lords and ladies to the great throne room on the morrow. They came eagerly whispering and talking and wondering who was to receive some new honor or fame.

When they were all gathered, the queen summoned a page to her throne and said, "I want you to ride through all the land and bring back to me all the weeds you can find. In the courtyard you will find saddled and waiting a coal black horse; mount and ride to the east." The page, dressed all in black, quickly left to do the queen's bidding.

Then the queen summoned a second page to her. He was dressed all in white.

The queen said, "I want you to ride through all this kingdom and bring back to me all the beautiful flowers you can find. There is a white horse ready and waiting in the courtyard; ride to the west."

As the horses hoofs died away in the distance the queen dismissed the courtiers. How they chattered and talked about what the queen meant by all this!

Many days passed and the event had been nearly forgotten when, one day, the queen again summoned her lords and ladies to the throne room.

The first page entered the room, his arms filled with vile and poisonous weeds. His hands were covered with heavy gloves with long gauntlets to protect them from the briers. He left his burden near the door and crossed the room to kneel before the queen, who asked, "What did you find on your journey?"

"Oh, Your Majesty, your kingdom is a kingdom of weeds and thorns. I did not know there were so many and such vile weeds. If something isn't done, your kingdom will be overrun."

"But did you find *no flowers?*" asked the queen.

"Flowers? Why, there must have been some flowers, but I didn't see them. You see, I was looking for weeds!"

Then the second page entered and his arms were filled with beautiful flowers—blossoms of every color of the rainbow—and their fragrance filled the entire room, as he crossed and laid them at the feet of the queen, who inquired, "And what did *you* find on your journey?"

"Oh, Your Majesty, your kingdom is a land of flowers. I did not know there were so many or such rare and lovely blossoms. Your country is one of beauty."

"But did you see no weeds?"

"Weeds? Why no; of course there must have been weeds, but I didn't see any. You see, *I* was *looking* for *flowers!*"

The queen turned to her courtiers. She had intended to make a little speech about finding what you look for in others and urging them to look for the beautiful things in life, but she saw that it was not necessary. Her lords and ladies with shamed faces and downcast eyes were all quietly leaving the courtroom. And ever after that the queen was happy as she ruled her loyal subjects wisely and well in that land of beauty.

—Adapted from a story by
Mrs. Elmer Adams.

(A story to stimulate family church attendance)

Master Jack was a bulldog puppy, just about so big. He had brown eyes and a black pug nose. He had funny little bows in his front legs. When he was dressed up to go to a birthday party, he wore a blue ribbon bow under his chin. He tried to be good. Sometimes he would stick out his tongue when he tried to talk, but for all that he was a very fine puppy.

When Master Jack reached the third grade he was the fastest runner in his class. Sometimes he would get himself dizzy turning in circles, trying to catch his tiny tail. He learned to do tricks such as standing on his head, turning somersaults, and jumping over sticks. He loved to play ball and to see how high he could jump. He played and ran hard all the long week when he was not in school, but on Sunday Master Jack had nothing to do.

One day Jack's mother said to Jack's father—who was a good old dog, snoozing by the fireplace—"Father, it seems to me we ought to take Jack to Sunday church school. It isn't right for him not to be brought up like all the good dogs in our neighborhood. I don't want my Jack to be a young heathen! After all, Jack, himself, wants to go to Sunday school because they have happy times there."

Jack's father said, "Well, Mother, if you will take Jack to Sunday school, I think it's a grand idea. I'll stay here and guard the house in case there's a fire or burglars."

That Saturday night Mother gave Jack such a scrubbing as he had never had before. She got a tub and put Jack into it. At first, he shivered while she poured water over his back and washed him all over with soap. She scrubbed behind Jack's ears. She washed his paws and trimmed his nails. It really made Jack feel good. On Sunday morning, looking shiny and clean, he said, "I want to go to Sunday school."

So Jack went to Sunday school every week. When Jack's birthday came, all the puppies in the department stood on their hind legs and sang "Happy Birthday to You." Jack took his birthday money from the pocket of his best red jacket, which he wore only on Sundays, and all the puppies cocked their ears to hear the coins tinkle, tinkle as Jack dropped them into the birthday bank. Jack, too, soon learned to join the songs and activities you call handwork but Jack's teacher called pawwork, and he had just the nicest and happiest time making a colored stained-glass window with the other puppies. Master Jack felt that he really belonged, because all the other puppies liked him, and his teacher was so wonderful. He trotted home from Sunday school with his Sunday school story paper in his mouth, wagging his stubby tail for joy, till it nearly fell off.

All the next week, Jack's mother helped him read his Sunday school home reading book of Bible stories. She was interested, too. Jack learned the memory verse, and he had an unusually good time in the department. He felt ashamed for the puppies who didn't try to learn the memory verse, and who had spent their money for candy, when they were supposed to have put it in the Sunday school offering. He was cross, too, at the puppies who always came to Sunday school late. Jack was always on time and tried to help his teacher by getting there early.

So it was that, on one fine Sunday morning, when dandelions had stopped blooming and their places had been taken by yellow buttercups and beautiful daisies, Jack's mother said to Jack's father, "Father, did you know that our Jack is being promoted today to the Junior Department in Sunday school? He is to take part in the Bible story dramatization in the Promotion Day program at our church." Now, when Jack's father heard that, he raised his head and pricked up his ears. "Mother," he asked, "do you mean to say that my Jack is going to have a speaking part at the puppies' promotion?" "That's just what I mean," said Jack's mother proudly. "Our Jack is on the program and he's a perfect wow. You know he's getting to be a big dog now."

Well, Jack's father shook himself, shaved off some of his longest whiskers, put on his best jacket and his spectacles and walked to church in his grandest manner with Mother and Master Jack. As Jack walked down the aisle and climbed the stairs with the other puppies to the platform, Jack's father leaned way over the end of the pew in order to get a good view of his own son Jack. When his turn came to speak, Jack stood on his hind legs, bowed to the right and left, rolled his eyes, made just the proper gesture with his paw, and never forgot a single word of his speech. He spoke loudly and clearly. All the older dogs in the congregation—the fathers and mothers—nodded to each other, when Jack finished, whispering behind their paws, "That was nice. Whose puppy is that?" And when some of the dogs whispered back, "Why, that's Mister Jack's puppy," Master Jack's father was so proud his neck began to swell way out until it nearly burst his brass-studded leather collar.

After church they all walked home together, little Jack carrying the red geranium plant which the teacher gave to all the puppies to take home on puppies' Promotion Day. Jack's father was feeling so grand he said, "I say, Mother, this Sunday school idea is pretty nice after all, isn't it? I believe I'll join Every Dog's Brotherhood Class, myself, so that I can go to Sunday school with Jack hereafter. I don't think he should have to go alone. Why don't you join the Ladies' Class?" "I'd love to," replied Jack's mother.

So now every Sunday there's really a sight to behold in that town. Jack's father, dressed in his finest, walks on one side; Jack's mother, looking very proud, with her nose tilted in the air, walks on the other side; and between them is Jack himself, wearing his blue ribbon bow and his best red jacket, all going down the street together to the church. As they pass by the houses, from the windows and from the verandas, the other dogs watch them go by—those careless dogs who have never been brought up properly and therefore often stay home from church. They are greatly impressed by this church-going family and they say to one another, "Well, we must admit that of all the dogs in this town, those three are the happiest dogs we know." And to that sentiment Jack, himself, who loves to go to Sunday school with his parents, responds with a proud and a loud "Bow wow!"

"DON'T BE ASHAMED TO PRAY!"

TOM BROWN'S FATHER sent him to a private boys' school when he was very young. At first it was hard to say good-by to his father and mother and go to live with many boys who were older than himself. His father, as he got on the train to go to school, shook hands with him and said, "Now, Tom, be a stouthearted boy and remember to study hard." His mother kissed him and said, "Don't forget to say your prayers each night." Tom bit his lip hard, for he didn't want to cry or show how badly he felt to be leaving home.

Some of the big boys were mean to Tom at first, but before long he was playing in all the sports at school and was making friends with other boys. As he grew older he became stronger and learned how to defend himself against the bullies at school. Tom thought he was a brave boy because he was good in sports and popular with all the other boys in the school.

One day a new boy named Arthur came to school. He was thin and shy and small for his age. The teacher said, "Tom, I am going to put Arthur in your charge. He is a new boy, and I want you to be a big brother to him and protect him. He will sleep in the dormitory with you in the same large room with a dozen other boys."

Tom was really unhappy. Physically, Arthur looked like a weakling. Tom only wanted friends who were powerful and strong and good in athletics.

Now when Tom had first come to the school and slept in the room with all those other boys, he did not get out of bed to say his prayers as he did at home. He was afraid the boys would make fun of him. So, after all the lights were out, he just pulled the sheets over his head and said his prayers to himself under the bed clothes. Then, after a while, he got tired of doing that and just went to sleep without even remembering to say his prayers.

The first night that the new boy, Arthur, came into the room he undressed just like the other boys did. But when he was in his pajamas, he quietly knelt down beside his bed to say his prayers, as he always had done at home. Three or four boys burst out laughing. Two or three others sneered, pointing their fingers at Arthur, and saying, "Look at the simple little idiot saying his prayers." Then over in the far corner of the room one of the boys who was a bully picked up his shoe, threw it across the room, and hit Arthur on the shoulder.

That was too much for Tom. He sprang out of bed. He picked up the shoe and threw it back. Then standing in the middle of the room, in a voice of indignation, he asked, "Is there anyone who wants to throw another shoe at Arthur?" All the boys quieted down. No one dared to say a word.

The lights were put out and everybody went to sleep, that is, everybody except Tom. Tom couldn't sleep because he was thinking. He had thought that Arthur was a weakling, yet Arthur had dared to say his prayers before the other boys and Tom had not. Tom had broken his promise to his mother, because he told her that he would always say his prayers. He felt very unhappy.

The next morning when Arthur knelt down to say his prayers, Tom knelt beside him, saying his prayers, too. No one laughed and no one sneered and no one threw any shoes. The room was very quiet. When Tom finished his prayers and looked up, he was surprised to see three other boys kneeling and saying their prayers, too. They had taken courage from Arthur and Tom!

GIVE SOMETHING

(Friendliness)

LINDA WAS A new girl in school, and she was rather shy. At first the girls had been friendly, but when she hurried home after school each day, offering no explanation, and taking no interest in them, they gradually let her alone.

"But I can't tell them I have to hurry home after school to baby-sit. They don't have to and they wouldn't understand," Linda said to herself. But way down deep Linda knew that she was partly ashamed, and that was why she was not friendly.

Linda's father was overseas and her mother, a nurse, left for work each day as soon as Linda came home, returning a little after eight at night. After her mother left, Linda took the twins for a walk in the park in the warm sunshine. Then she got them their supper and

put them to bed.

It was almost time for her mother to return one night when Linda got out her scrapbook and pasted some poems in it that she had cut from her Sunday school papers. Turning the leaves slowly, she found a poem she had put in a long time before. The words seemed to jump right out at her: "Give something of yourself—"

And suddenly Linda's face grew warm thinking of the many times she had walked away from the girls; and how she had never offered to clean erasers after school, or taken any interest in her schoolroom.

"Tomorrow I'll be friendly," she promised herself. "I'll tell them I baby-sit and I'll help clean erasers at recess." She went to bed then, feeling good inside.

When Linda walked into her classroom next morning a group of girls stood by the blackboard talking.

"Hi," Linda called gaily, as if that were her usual morning greeting.

"Hello," they answered. Then, "What do you know!" one of the girls whispered loudly.

All day her attempts to be friendly met with no success. Lingering a moment after school, hoping to walk down the steps with some of the girls, she was again disappointed, for they brushed past her, talking and laughing.

Linda hurried on home, then, and took her small brothers to play in the park. She also tried to keep an eye on a small boy who wanted to climb a large oak tree.

When Linda started for home with the twins, she heard a cry for help from the oak tree, where the small boy sat almost at the top, crying.

"What's the matter?" she called.

"I can't get down," he wailed.

Linda almost said, "I told you not to climb up there," *when she remembered!* She could help him, and that was "giving something"—

"Stand right there while I climb the tree," she told her brothers. "I won't be long."

She helped the boy down, and when his feet touched the ground, he scurried away like a frightened squirrel.

Linda was almost down, when she stepped on a dry branch that snapped, and before she could catch a limb to cling to she tumbled out of the tree. She limped home and called her mother. In a little while her mother came bringing a doctor. He examined her foot and told her she had sprained it and would probably miss a day or two of school.

Next morning Linda called her teacher and told her why she would be absent. Then she lay down on a davenport in the living room, watching the twins.

The day was the longest she had ever known. Glancing at the clock once, she thought, "School is out now and everybody will be going to Marion's party." Linda felt so badly not to be invited.

Then suddenly, above the twins' noisy play, Linda heard her name. Coming across the lawn were all the boys and girls in her schoolroom.

Linda's mother hurried from the kitchen and opened the door.

"Surprise!" they shouted, swarming into the large room, depositing two cartons of ice cream, frosted cakes, candy, and paper plates and spoons on the table.

Linda could not speak.

"We didn't know you baby-sat every day after school until teacher told us," Elva smiled shyly. "I'm an expert sitter, and I'd like to help you, if you'll let me."

"I would love it," Linda answered, wondering why she had ever thought they would not understand.

Marion came out from the kitchen carrying a basket of flowers and set them on a table beside Linda.

"Jackie lives next door to Elva and he told her how you helped him down from the tree. It was wonderful." Marion looked down at the floor. "We thought you were different, Linda, and—"

They all crowded around Linda. "We missed you today."

Linda smiled. "I missed everyone, too." She looked at the smiling, friendly faces of her new-found friends, and realized that she would not be lonely any more.

—Adapted from a story by
Marie A. Morrison, in *Juniors*.

FOLLOW THE LEADER

(*Obedience*)

NANCY'S MOTHER knew that streets are very dangerous places for children, because automobiles go whizzing along there at such high speed. And Nancy's mother loved her little girl so dearly, that every day, when she buttoned up her coat, as she was getting ready to go to school, she would say, "Now, Nancy, remember, never, never walk or play in the street. Always keep on the sidewalk."

And Nancy, who by this time was getting just a trifle weary of being told the same thing over and over again, replied, "But, Mommy, I never do walk or play in the street."

Nancy was a good little girl, and she never thought of disobeying her mother. But deep down inside, she often felt tempted to try walking in the street.

But every time she was tempted, she would hear in her conscience her mother's voice saying firmly, "Now, Nancy, remember never, never walk or play in the street."

One day there was a very hard thundershower. The rain poured down in sheets and floods.

On her way home from school that day, though the shower was over, Nancy saw great pools of water left standing on the sidewalks. Nancy didn't like to get her new shoes wet in the puddles, though she often waded in puddles barefoot.

Just then she looked up and saw Mr. Jones, who lived across the street from her house, and whom she liked very much. And Mr. Jones was walking in the middle of the street.

"Why don't you walk on the sidewalk, Mr. Jones, like I do?" asked Nancy.

"Well, my dear little girl, you see, there are so many puddles on the sidewalk, that I find it much easier to walk here in the street where it is dry."

"May I come out there and walk in the street with you, Mr. Jones?" asked Nancy.

"Why, yes, of course," said her kind friend and neighbor.

Nancy walked right behind Mr. Jones in the street, trying to keep in his big steps. "I just love this," she giggled. "Isn't it fun, Mr.   101

Jones? I never did it before, because my mommy doesn't like me to walk in the street."

"How interesting!" answered Mr. Jones absent-mindedly. You see, Mr. Jones was walking along and thinking his own thoughts, and hardly hearing a word of what Nancy was saying.

"Yes," Nancy went on. "My mommy tells me about a dozen times a day, 'Never, never walk or play in the street,' but it is all right, isn't it, Mr. Jones?"

Then suddenly Mr. Jones heard what the little girl was saying. "Come, Nancy," he said very quickly. "Let's both get right back on the sidewalk. Your mother is so right. She has trained you to be careful. And not by a careless act of mine will I break down all her fine teaching."

"But she won't care," offered Nancy.

"Oh, yes, she will," replied Mr. Jones. "Your mother is just right, and you have taught me something, too, Nancy. I'll tell you what," said Mr. Jones. "Let's play 'Follow the Leader.' I'll walk on the sidewalk and you follow me." And so they did.

And though Nancy often saw Mr. Jones many, many times after that, she never did see him walking in the street again.

POOR LOSER

(*The sin of cheating*)

"OH, DEAR, Kathy is winning again!" Patsy thought.

"Don't make such a long face, Patsy!" laughed Kathy. "It's only a game we decided to play on this rainy afternoon, remember? Maybe you'll win the next game."

"Maybe," agreed Patsy. "Now if only the spinner will stop at six! That's what I need to put my man back."

She spun, but the needle stopped at five, not six. Then a naughty thought jumped into Patsy's mind. Kathy was looking hard at the board, trying to figure out which of her men to move next. She wouldn't see if—

"Oh, but that wouldn't be fair!" thought Patsy. "Still, it's only a little thing, and I don't want Kathy telling at school tomorrow how she came to my house and beat me every game." Patsy just touched the needle and it moved from five to six.

Kathy looked up. "See you got your six, Patsy! Now I must decide how to play to catch that man again."

"Ummm-m, huh," mumbled Patsy.

It was easier to cheat the second time. A few minutes later Patsy changed the needle again. And so she won a game.

Kathy wanted to play another game, but suddenly Patsy didn't feel like playing. The parcheesi game was no longer fun. Kathy was surprised, because Patsy wasn't gay and cheerful any longer. Soon Kathy went home.

That night as Patsy was going over her reading lesson she came across the word "cheat," and it made her jump.

"The needle on the spinner moved so quickly this afternoon that it didn't seem like anything. But I won't do it again ever!" Patsy said to herself.

She meant that, too, for she knew that those who are trying to follow Jesus, as she was, shouldn't do even "little things" that were wrong. Patsy felt a little queer when she said her prayers that night, and so she hurried through them instead of taking time to tell Jesus how much she loved him, and to thank God for all his goodness to her that day.

Later that week Patsy had a chance to play more games. Another friend, Alma, invited her over to her house to play with her new neighbors, Don and Winifred. And the first thing Patsy knew she found herself cheating again, just so she could win the game of "A Trip to England to See the Queen." Patsy was afraid Don had seen her pick up just the right card she needed to win.

While they were all eating candy, Alma invited Don and Winifred to go to church school with them the next Sunday.

But Don answered, "Our family doesn't go to church regularly. You see, it seems to me that many Christians are no better than the people who do not go to church."

The little group broke up soon and Patsy wasn't at all sorry, for she felt so miserable. She had made Don think there wasn't any use in going to church school and knowing Jesus, and she had had a dreadful time.

"It was fun up to the time I cheated," thought Patsy on the way home. "Why did I do it again?"

The next morning when Patsy awoke, she slipped out of bed and 103

knelt beside it. "Dear God, help me to be brave enough to own up
to the wrong I have done," Patsy prayed. Now a peaceful feeling came
over her. God would help. She had the courage to do what was right.

When Alma and Winifred came to school, Patsy began: "I really
didn't win that game yesterday. I cheated. Don saw me, I'm sure, and
so he thinks that Christians aren't any different from other boys and
girls. That isn't true, Don, because Alma and Kathy play fair. And
God will help me to after this, like he helped me to confess. I just
didn't want to lose, and I forgot that cheating isn't winning anyway."

"No, Patsy," spoke up Don. "I really didn't see you cheat. But there
must be something very worth while about being a follower of Jesus
and knowing that you can talk things over with God and receive his
help when you need it."

"Let's forget the Sunday comics, Don, and go to church school
with Patsy, Alma, and the rest," urged Winifred.

"And in the afternoon come over to my house," invited Patsy, "and
we'll play something—fair!"

—Adapted from a story by
Grace Helen Davis, in *Juniors*.

THE FIREMAN'S BROTHER

(A story of courage)

DICK NEELY was smaller than anyone else in his class.

"Here, you Runt! Get going. We're going to play baseball. Go
home and change your clothes and be in the park in half an hour."
That was the way Hank Norris, the biggest fellow in the class, bossed
Dick around.

Dick pushed open the door of the apartment house where he lived.
His big brother Ed was standing there. He was six feet tall, with
wide shoulders and strong legs. He was training at the New York
City Fireman's School.

"Hi, Ed, how come you're home so early today?"

"Just to give you a workout," grinned Ed. "Shall we go to the
park?"

104   Ed was a wonderful brother. He never talked about Dick's small

size, and he taught him exercises to make his muscles hard and firm.

"I promised the kids I'd play baseball," said Dick, "but they can get along without me."

"No sir," answered Ed. "We Neelys have to keep our word. Think they'll let me in on the game?"

Of course it was wonderful having Ed play with the gang. He could pitch circles around the other fellows and even Hank Norris had to take second place. Dick was sure no one would ever call him Runt again. But the next day was just the same.

"Say, Runt, that's some brother you got. You'd never know you were in the same family," said Hank.

One day Ed took Dick to visit the fireman's school. He saw where they did their exercises and where they practiced climbing ladders. He saw the different-sized dummies the firemen carried. And Ed even taught him how to carry one with the fireman's carry.

That night Dick dreamed of fire engines and woke up to hear real sirens. He jumped out of bed, ran into his brother Ed's room. "Step on it if you want to come with me," said Ed, who was nearly dressed.

When they got to the fire, Ed hurried on to help the firemen, but Dick stayed with the other watchers. On the lawn, a man and woman and a little girl with coats over their pajamas were telling some grownups how they had escaped from the house just in time. There was a bunch of kids standing around, but the only one Dick knew was Hank Norris.

Suddenly the little girl screamed. "Daddy!! Butch is in the cellar."

The father put his arm around the little girl. "I know, honey, but we can't risk our lives to rescue a dog. Maybe he'll get out all right."

"Hank," Dick gasped. "There's a live dog in that cellar."

Hank shrugged his shoulder. "Can I help it?"

Dick hesitated only a moment. Then he dashed across the lawn and pushed the cellar window open. He fastened it with its hook and jumped down into the cellar. He landed with a thud, and a sharp pain shot up his leg. He groped his way through the darkness until he found the limp little dog. Then he put him across his shoulders in a real fireman's carry, and crawled back to the window. Standing on a chair which he dragged to the window, he managed to shove Butch out onto the lawn. Then he managed to wriggle himself through the window. He lay on the cold ground, gasping for air.

Just then strong arms lifted him and a well-loved voice said, "Take it easy, fireman." Dick leaned against his brother's strong chest and knew nothing more until he was in his own bed.

It was two days before Dick could go back to school. His father drove him down because he could hardly walk with his sprained ankle.

All the boys came running to meet him except Hank.

"How did you do it, Dick?"

"Weren't you scared?"

"How did you ever get out?"

Everyone was talking at once. No one called him Runt. Then someone said, "Why didn't anyone help you, Dick? Weren't any of the other kids there?"

Dick looked across at Hank who stood behind the others with his head bent low.

Then Hank replied for him: "Guess it was lucky Dick was there because none of the rest of us would have had the courage to do what Dick did."

Dick and Hank smiled at each other with perfect understanding.

Just then the school bell rang. No one ran up the steps of the school. The boys were walking slowly today for their new leader, Dick, limped along with a cane.

—Adapted from a story by
Catherine Marshall, in *Juniors.*

A STORY OF GRATITUDE FOR SIMPLE NEEDS

(An object talk on gratitude)

HERE IS A LOAF of bread. Think, do you know how much it weighs? How many slices are there in a loaf of bread? How many jelly sandwiches can you make from one loaf? How many loaves of bread can you make from one bushel of wheat? How many loaves of bread do the bakers in America make each day? Then when you think of the farmer who raises the wheat grains that make the flour that make the bread that you eat for breakfast, how much does the farmer get paid as his share of the price for a loaf of bread? How daily is our daily bread? (You know, we pray, "Give us this day our daily bread.")

Each loaf of bread is supposed by law to weigh one pound and each loaf is supposed to have sixteen slices of bread. You can quickly see that each loaf would make you eight sandwiches.

The baker can make sixty-eight loaves of bread from a bushel of wheat, but all the bakers in America each day make about forty million loaves of bread. Wouldn't that make an enormous pile of bread if the loaves were all stacked up in a great pyramid? Just think how many slices of bread there would be, six billion, four hundred million, and the daily bread in America would make three billion, two hundred million sandwiches.

Think how many kinds of bread there are to help us enjoy eating our daily bread. There is white bread, enriched white bread with vitamins, whole-wheat bread, wheat bread, pumpernickel bread, rye bread, graham bread, cracked wheat bread, and then you know there are the long funny-shaped loaves of bread called French bread, and there is the bread with the hard crust called Italian bread.

Many boys and girls like raisin bread. Did you ever count how many raisins there are in a slice of raisin bread? Well, try it sometime. The baker cannot cheat you on the number of raisins he puts in each loaf. The United States loaf requirements are to put fifty pounds of raisins for every one hundred pounds of flour used to make bread. Raisin bread would not be much good, would it, if you only found two in a loaf? Then you would wonder if your sister got all the raisins or your older brother.

When you go to the store, you may pay eighteen or nineteen cents for a loaf of bread. Would you like to know how many people have to get some pay out of the eighteen or nineteen cents that you pay?

Well, the grocer takes two cents for having the loaf of bread ready for you to take home. The baker takes eleven cents for mixing the flour, baking the loaf, and putting it in cellophane. The big buildings where they store the grain known as elevators and the railroad trains that carry the flour to the baker take one cent for each loaf. The miller or the man who grinds the kernels of wheat grain into flour takes one cent out of each loaf, while the farmer gets just three and one half cents for all the trouble of plowing the land, sowing the seed, tilling the soil, reaping the grain and storing it in the barns.

But there is one thing that is free about the loaf of bread. It is the sunshine and the rain and the earth which together by God's goodness make the wheat grow from the seed, so that we truly can cay with Maltbie D. Babcock:

> "Back of the loaf is the snowy flour,
>   Back of the flour the mill;
> Back of the mill the wheat, the show'r,
>   The sun and our Father's will."

A MODERN PRODIGAL SON

(*Adapted for juvenile delinquents*)

BOB LIVED ON a large farm with his parents and an older brother. His very rich father was growing old and had promised to divide his money with his sons. Now Bob was always hearing about the excitement of city life. He'd seen it on television and read about it in comics and magazines. So he became impatient for his share of the money. He wanted to enjoy city life while he was young.

"Dad, can I have my share of your money now?" Bob asked one night.

"Why—why I suppose so. Why do you want it?" questioned the father.

"Well," Bob hesitated, and tried to wipe the sweat from his hands without being seen, "I—I'd like to know just how much I have. I can't decide if I want to go to college or start in business right away."

"I can't see your need for it, Bob, but if that's what you want, I'll give it to you. I do hope you'll think before you spend it or use it foolishly." His father got up and started for the door.

Bob smiled to himself. "If he thinks I'm going to be careful, he's crazy," Bob thought, "I want to have fun. No college or business for me. I want to see the city. I want to live."

A few nights later Bob slipped away from home. He was tired of farm life. He wanted to get away from his "good" brother. He was tired of hearing, "Why can't you be good like your brother?" He wanted to be himself and have adventure.

The city was larger than Bob had ever dreamed! At night it was a blaze of lights that glittered against the ink-black sky; lights that flashed on and off and sparkled like diamonds. He met young people in the restaurants and drugstores. He spoke to people in the parks and on the streets, and soon he had a group of friends. He had enough money for everyone. They went to night clubs and had big parties in ritzy hotels. They saw the big shows, ball games, fights and wrestling matches. Bob hired fast motorboats and gave midnight cruises. They danced and laughed and drank champagne. Bob even bought a new French car and roared up and down the narrow streets, screeching through red lights. Whenever he threw a party all his friends were eager to come.

But before he knew it, Bob's money was all gone! The day came when he had to go out looking for a job. None of his friends helped him get work. They forgot him.

"I'll soon save a lot of money and then they'll come back," Bob thought as he worked.

Now he began to spend his nights in taprooms. He spent the long nights drinking beer and watching fights on the television. When he talked to the people in the taproom, they got mad because they were drunk. Even the television made him unhappy when he remembered how he used to sit in ringside seats. His money and friends were gone. Did real friends run away and forget you when you needed them most? The ones he had known on the farm back home never had.

Hard times came. Bob lost his job and couldn't find another. He had no money for food or for rent, so he was thrown out of his room. He began to sneak down alleys and search the garbage cans for scraps of food.

Winter came and the park bench was too cold to sleep on. He

found a big packing box in a dump near the wharves. He curled up there at night in its shelter.

One night when Bob came to the dump the box was gone. Now he had nothing. He thought of jumping off the pier and drowning himself, but he didn't quite dare.

He sat down on the pier, pulled his torn coat around him, and leaned against the cold pilings and tried to sleep. His body was so tired it hurt to move, but he couldn't sleep. The pains in his stomach were unbearable, for he hadn't eaten all day. He hated the friends that had spent his money and then all deserted him. He hated the lights. He shivered and tried to forget the dirty streets and the crowded, sweaty, smoke-filled bars. He thought of the big white farmhouse with its yellow-lighted windows, as he kicked at the dirty wharf rat running through the slush on the pier. He thought of his warm room at home. Even the cows in the red barn were warmer than he was, and he wished he could go back.

The blue star-dotted sky over the farm seemed so beautiful as he remembered it. He closed his eyes to shut out the flashy all-night-long lights of the city. Out there were his family and his true friends. All his thoughts seemed to say, "Go home!"

"But I can't," he cried half out loud, and started to sit up. "Dad would never take me back now. He'd hate me. He'd ask me what I did with the money, and I can't tell him, I can't—I can't." He sank back shivering and weeping, holding his wet, torn coat as close as he could.

Then he remembered his father's hired men. "They have homes, and food, and clothes," he thought grudgingly. Suddenly he sat up. "Why couldn't I ask Dad for a job as a hired man? I don't deserve to be his son, but he might give me a job and let me earn my living. There's nothing left for me here. I'll go back and ask for a job on my father's farm."

A few days later Bob stumbled up the dark winding lane. The icy wind blew through his ragged clothes and his legs ached until he felt he could not take another step, but with the house in view he started to run. He ran only a few steps and then he stopped, shivering and afraid. What would his father do? Perhaps he should never have come. Perhaps he should go back now.

As he waited in the snow under the black leafless trees, afraid and alone, the door opened and someone came out. It was his father, and he was looking off into the distance as if he were expecting someone.

Bob wanted to call him, to wave his arms in welcome, but he was afraid.

Suddenly his father saw him. As he watched, his father ran down the road to meet him, and he realized that it was he himself that his father had been looking for. His father threw his arms around him and kissed him, although he was dirty and unshaven and in rags. He held him so tightly that Bob thought his ribs would break. His father was so happy to see him that he cried.

"Dad, Dad," Bob sobbed as soon as he could catch his breath, "I don't deserve to be your son any more. I—I don't ask you to take me back, but you do hire men—could you—could you hire me? I'd work very hard."

"No, Bob, no," his father smiled through his tears, "you are always my son."

He took Bob into the house and gave him a hot shower. He gave him a new suit, bought especially for his return. He had new shoes and he took his ring off his hand and placed it on Bob's, and promised him that he never would be anything but his son. He never even asked about the money Bob had wasted in the city.

That night there was a big dinner for Bob. The biggest turkey on the farm was on the table and all Bob's favorite food. The neighbors were there and all of Bob's old friends. The house blazed with lights and the singing echoed over the snowy fields. Bob was placed at the head of the table and his father announced before the whole crowd that he was proud to claim his son that was lost, but now was found.

—Charles Waugaman

A Modern Prodigal Son

111

special day stories

THE FIFTH COMMANDMENT
(A Father's Day talk)

SAM KNEW ALL the Ten Commandments. He could recite them without missing a word. But there was one commandment he tried very hard to forget. That was the Fifth Commandment, which says, "Honor your father and your mother."

Sam's father was poor. His father was a book peddler. And Sam was ashamed of his father's poverty and of his life as a book peddler.

Now Sam lived in England about two hundred years ago. On market days Sam's father would pack his books into a wheelbarrow and wheel them along the road. The wheel went *squeak, squeak, squeak* until the father came to the public square of the town of Lichfield. Here, as the crowds of people passed by, he would stand and shout, "Read a good book. Buy a fine book. Take home a book to read. Please buy a book today."

One day Sam's father fell sick. He could not move off the bed. He called his son, Sam, to him and said, "Sam, my lad, I'm too sick to go about peddling my books today. Will you please push my wheelbarrow and books and stand with them in the public square? Stand there in your father's place, will you, my son, and ask people to buy a book?"

"I don't want to," pouted Sam.

"But we need the money, my boy, to buy bread and meat to eat and wood to keep us warm," said the father.

"I don't care what happens," said Sam angrily. "I won't do it," and he went out and slammed the door .with a hateful bang. He was ashamed to let any of his schoolmates know that his father was a poor peddler.

Very soon after that Sam's father died.

The years went by and Sam grew to be a brilliant and famous man. He wrote books and edited the first great English dictionary. Every-

112

*The Fifth
Commandment*

where in England, people bowed low before the great Doctor Samuel
Johnson.

But try as he would, Dr. Johnson could never forget that Fifth Commandment, "Honor your father and your mother," and the sad way
he had broken that commandment when he was a boy.

Then one rainy day everyone in the public square of the town of
Lichfield was surprised to see a man standing out in the rain beside
a wheelbarrow. He was the now world-famous Dr. Samuel Johnson.
On the very spot where his father used to stand as a book peddler,
Dr. Johnson now stood very solemnly, with his head uncovered to
the rain, his hat in hand, bowing low to say by this very act that he
wished to acknowledge his wrong.

113

The people gathered about to watch the famous man. He stood there for over an hour while the rain pelted down upon him. Then he spoke to the crowd. He told them how once, more than fifty years ago, he had dishonored his father and broken the fifth of God's great Commandments. Filled with shame and remorse, Dr. Johnson now stood there in repentance to pay a public tribute to his noble father.

And as the people looked closer they saw that Dr. Samuel Johnson's face was not only wet with the rain, but that his cheeks were wet with the scalding tears of bitter remorse. And the people loved him because a famous man had been willing to admit publicly his sin, and had done what he could to show how much he still loved and honored his father.

DAN AND ZEKE

(A story for Universal Bible Sunday)

BOB'S AND PATSY'S father was driving them through the White Mountains in New Hampshire one July day.

"Now that we have seen the Old Man of the Mountain," Bob said, referring to the great stone image of a man's face made by the wind cutting the rocks high up on the mountain, "where do we go next and what will we see?"

"Well," said Dad, who always wanted his children to know something about the great men of our country, "how would you like to visit a little farmhouse on one of the country roads through the woods, if I promise to tell you a story about a famous American who was born there?"

"I would," said Patsy, "if you tell us his name."

"I would, too," said Bob, "if you will tell us something about him when he was a boy."

"Simple enough," said Dad. "The story is really about Daniel, although I must also tell you a little about his brother Ezekiel. I suppose you know that here in New England, in the early days of our country's history, parents usually gave Bible names to their children."

Just then the automobile gave a lurch around the corner, went over a bump in the road, and came to a stop in the dirt driveway which led to an old red, weather-beaten farmhouse.

"Now this is the farm where Daniel was born and grew up," said Dad. "You can see that his father was a very poor farmer. He and his boys, Daniel and Ezekiel, had to work very hard from sunup to sundown each day trying to scrabble a living off this rocky land and thin soil.

"Daniel soon saw that he wouldn't go very far, for he had great ambition, if he always lived on this farm. He would just grow up to be a poor farmer on a poor farm. Daniel wanted to go to college and become a great man for his country. Just to make sure that his father knew that he intended to make something of himself someday, Daniel painted a sign on a board and nailed it up in the cherry tree near the barn where his father would read it. This is what the sign said: 'I will not always be a farmer.'

"Daniel dreamed of leading men, of speaking before great audiences, and of going to our nation's capital as a statesman. But he was a regular boy with his share of mischievousness in his make-up. One day his father had left some work for Ezekiel and Daniel to do on the farm. The father came back and found that his boys had not done the work.

"'What have you been doing, Ezekiel?' asked the father angrily.

"'Nothing, sir,' answered Zeke.

"The father then turned to Daniel. 'Well, Daniel,' he asked, 'what have you been doing?'

"'Helping Zeke,' said Daniel with a grin.

"The father laughed, too, and set the boys to work.

"Daniel's teacher found him very bright in school in more ways than one. One day the teacher saw how dirty Daniel's hand was. He called him to his desk before the whole school and said, 'Hold out your right hand.' Daniel held out his right hand to receive the hard blows of the teacher's rattan.

"'Daniel,' said the teacher, 'if you can show me anywhere in this world any hand dirtier than your right hand, I will let you off.'

"Daniel immediately pulled out his other hand from behind his back and showed that to the teacher. He got off.

"Early in life Daniel came to know the Bible well. And one reason why he became a great orator was because he knew the Bible so well and loved it. His teacher, Mr. Tappen, taught the Bible in the

115

country schoolhouse. One Friday the teacher asked his scholars to try to see how many Bible verses they could commit to memory by Monday morning.

"Daniel recited over seventy verses. When the teacher said that was more than enough, Daniel was crestfallen, for he had a dozen more chapters he had memorized to recite. The teacher was amazed.

"Daniel so loved the Bible that he liked to memorize whole chapters and psalms. As a boy, Daniel became such a fine reader of the Bible that in the country hotels or inns nearby, the overnight guests and the teamsters as they pulled up to the door would say, 'Come, let us go inside and hear Daniel recite us some psalms.'

"Because he was so keen-minded, Daniel saw how interesting and beautiful the Bible is. He made its language and verses a part of his everyday speech as a citizen, a lawyer, and a great orator. When he became America's most famous orator, he said, 'If there is anything in my style or thoughts to be commended, the credit is due my kind parents who instilled into my mind at an early age a love of the Scriptures.' "

"But what was Daniel's last name?" Bob asked his father.

"Yes," said Patsy, "you haven't told us who Daniel became."

"Sure enough," said Dad. "This was Daniel Webster, one of America's greatest senators, orators, and statesmen. His fame spread far and wide over America, but though he became so famous, he never lost his love for the Bible. And in his last will and testament he ordered written on his tombstone words expressing his undying love for the Book: "Lord, I Believe: Help Thou My Unbelief."

THE LEGEND OF THE HUMAN PYRAMID

(A Rally Day story)

THIS IS RALLY DAY when we are all returning to Sunday church school wearing our Sunday-best clothes and feeling so happy to be in our classes again. Right down there in the Primary Department, I can see a girl who has on her best dress, and over there a girl who has a pair of brand-new shoes, and there is a boy who remembered to bring his Bible.

I want to tell you a story about some people in a town long, long ago and far, far away who had something happen to them that was very wonderful.

One bright morning, as the people of the town were looking up, there came down from the sky, hanging by a silver thread, an immense golden ball. It rested there in the air suspended just above the people's heads. It seemed they could reach up and almost touch it, if only they were tall enough.

Right after the golden ball came down from the sky, the people saw a white-winged angel flying about blowing a golden trumpet, and saying to the people of the town, "If you will reach up and touch this golden ball, wonderful things will happen to you. This town will become rich, receiving a great blessing, and you will be happier than all the other towns in the world."

As soon as the angel went away, the news and excitement spread through the streets and houses of the town. People came running from everywhere to see the golden ball shining and turning in the sunlight above their heads.

"Let me touch the ball first," each one cried. "No, I want to touch it first," said others. So they pushed and they pushed and they jostled and they jostled as the crowd grew bigger and bigger.

Men pushed the women out of the way saying, "Get over there, this is a man's job."

The women in turn kicked the men in the shins saying, "I'll teach you big bullies to push us away."

Then a high school boy, who was on the football team, made a dash and charged into the crowd, knocking over some people, and some girls slapped his face for him. The crowd was fighting and getting angrier every minute, trying to reach up their hands toward the golden ball. But alas and alack no one was tall enough to get his hands, even when they were stretched to the utmost, close to the golden ball.

When they saw, at last, how hopeless it was for any of them to touch the golden ball, someone in the crowd said, "Let's find the tallest man in the town. Perhaps he could reach it for us and bring down the great blessing upon our town."

So they sent messengers throughout the town and, at last, way out on the outskirts of the town, far, far out, they found a farmer who was very, very tall. In fact, he was a giant, seven feet tall. He owned

117

a farm where he raised hundreds of heads of green lettuce for the market, so they nicknamed him "Lettuce." His last name was Rally— and it "rally" was—so they called him "Lettuce Rally."

When Lettuce Rally heard the news of the golden ball, he came running as fast as he could. The crowd made way for him, and he reached his arms way, way up, then he stretched his fingers to the utmost, then he stood on tiptoe, but still his hands could not quite reach the golden ball.

The crowd groaned with disappointment. Some said, "There, I knew he could never reach that golden ball." Others said, "What's the use, it was no good having Lettuce Rally here. It's the same old thing, it just can't be done. This golden ball is beyond our reach."

Then Lettuce Rally, who stood head and shoulders above the crowd, said, "Stop this shouting and this nonsense. We can touch that golden ball, if you will do what I say, and I will show you how we can do it." Now the people were ready to obey Lettuce Rally.

He said, "Twenty strong men come here, stand shoulder to shoulder, and lock arms together. I want a solid base of men." Twenty strong men almost glued themselves together. "Now," said Lettuce Rally, "I want ten young men to climb up on their shoulders, locks arms, and stand on the shoulders of these men." Leaping up like squirrels, ten young men stood on the shoulders of the men below. "Now, I want five boys of high school age to shinny up and stand on the shoulders of the ten young men," said Lettuce Rally. The five boys from high school stood on the shoulders of the others. They were making a human pyramid.

They were getting nearer and nearer to the ball now, but still they could not quite reach it. Then Lettuce Rally said, "Now give me a little child." He picked up a little girl who was of primary age, and he handed her to the men on the ground, who handed her to the men of the next height, hand over hand until she stood on the shoulders of the topmost boy, who held her firmly by her legs. Then the little girl reached up her arms. The people were breathless. Her arms did not reach the golden ball. Then she unfolded her fingers, and her longest finger just touched the golden ball.

Suddenly there came down a shower of the most beautiful stars you can imagine. They were shining stars of purest gold. There were stars for everyone in the town and for the men of the pyramid, and the little girl. They all went home singing, rich and happy, because they had stood together to help the little child reach up toward the shining golden ball. That day a child had been lifted toward God—and far off all the people heard bells in heaven ringing for joy.

SUSAN'S BLOOD TRANSFUSION

(A Communion Sunday story)

"WHO'S SICK AT your house?" asked Ted across the street of his pal Jim. "I saw the doctor's car at your house this morning."

"It's my kid sister Susan," said her older brother slowly. "She was racing downhill with Mary when she fell on the concrete sidewalk scraping her knee. The doctor said that she must have got some dirt into the wound, for now she has blood poisoning."

"That's too bad," offered Ted. "She's only six years old. I hope they won't have to send her to the hospital."

"That's what makes me feel low this morning, Ted. The doctor said she must be rushed to the hospital for a blood transfusion."

"What's that?" asked Ted who was two years younger than Jim.

"Well, it's something like this. Some people have bad blood or poisoned blood, see, and they will die unless they can get some good blood pumped into them. Someone, I guess, who has good blood gives up theirs for the person who is going to die, and that saves him and he gets well."

"You mean someone will have to give his very own blood to save Susan?" asked Ted.

"That's what the doctor says."

"I wouldn't want to give up my blood. I wouldn't want to die," said Ted, who was afraid.

"You might," protested Jim bravely, "if it was someone you loved a whole lot."

Just then Jim's mother called. "The doctor wants us all to come to the hospital at once to take samples of our blood. Come with us, Jim, in the car. One of us may need to give our blood to save Susan's life."

Jim jumped into the car, and soon they were in the hospital walking down the corridor toward the laboratory. Here the nurse took a sample of Jim's blood and typed it.

119

A little later Jim, his father and mother were sitting in the waiting room at the hospital when the doctor came in with his white, starched coat on. He walked over and put his hand on Jim's shoulder.

"Jim, we have taken samples of the blood of all the members of your family, and yours is the only blood that matches Susan's. Will you give your blood to save your sister Susan's life?"

Jim stood up trembling, his teeth set tight with determination and said, "Yes, sir."

"Come with me then," said the doctor, who took him away with him down the long corridors into a room where there were beds.

Jim was only twelve years old and he had never before been in a hospital. They put Jim on a couch and attached a tube to his arm to let the blood flow out of his body into a big bottle. As Jim was lying there on the bed, the doctor noticed that Jim was growing paler and paler. There was really no reason why Jim should look so white. And then the doctor realized that Jim was frightened.

So the doctor said, "Jim, you're not feeling badly, are you?"

"No, sir," said Jim trying to be brave. "But I was wondering just how long it would be before I die."

"Die?" exclaimed the doctor. "Oh, Jim, did you think that people who gave their blood to others must die?"

"Yes, sir," said Jim, and he couldn't quite hold back the tears.

"Well," said the doctor, "you are not going to die. Don't worry. You are going to live, but you were willing to give up everything if you could save your sister Susan; and that means you are a fine, brave man."

Jim was glad when he got off the couch and found that he was standing on his own feet and he was really still alive. But he kept thinking about what he had been through, and how he did give some of his blood to save his sister's life.

One Sunday at church he was still thinking about it as he sat in the pew. When he heard the minister read the verse of the hymn which he announced for everybody to sing, it was a hymn Jim knew well, but somehow it had a new meaning for him today:

> "There is a green hill far away,
> Without a city wall,
> Where the dear Lord was crucified,
> Who died to save us all.

Special Day Stories

120

O dearly, dearly has He loved!
And we must love Him too,
And trust in His redeeming blood,
And try His works to do."
                    —*Cecil Frances Alexander*

WHO THANKS BEST?

(*A Thanksgiving Sunday story*)

JUST A WEEK before Thanksgiving Day, there hung in a bank window in Bostontown a beautiful painting of the Pilgrims for all the passers-by to see. It was, as you have guessed, a painting of a Pilgrim family eating the Thanksgiving meal about the wooden table in their log cabin.

The table was bare of even a tablecloth. There was a big wooden bowl in the center filled with hot, steaming turkey stew. Pilgrims then, you know, were poor and food was often scarce in the winter.

At one end of the oblong table sat the stern Pilgrim father with his beard, and at the other end the Pilgrim mother with her gray hood over her head. Between them on both sides of the table sat the older children, and in the center of the picture sat a chubby Pilgrim baby in her high chair with her clean white bib tied about her neck.

Although the table had only one dish of food and no white linen tablecloth, no china dishes, and no silver, but only wooden forks and spoons and pewter plates on the bare polished board, still the Pilgrims were not forgetting to be thankful to God. Before eating one least bit of their food, they waited for prayer. The Pilgrim father, inviting his wife and children and the baby to bow their heads reverently, was saying a prayer of blessing for the food and giving thanks to God, the bountiful heavenly Father.

Now it was a very long prayer. The Pilgrims had a habit of saying long prayers, sometimes even as long as one half-hour. Many children found it hard to wait through the long prayer before they could begin to eat their dinner. While this Pilgrim father prayed, you could see his fine but stern face long, sad, and solemn.

121

At the opposite end of the table the seated Pilgrim mother was trying hard to listen patiently to the long prayer, even though she knew that her steaming stew in the wooden bowl was getting colder by the minute. She kept her hands folded on the edge of the table and her eyes tightly shut. She, too, was being faithful to this solemn duty of thanksgiving, even by means of a long prayer.

But the Pilgrim baby in her high chair, with her white bib on, was another story. She had her own ideas. Perhaps she tried at first to be good, to bow her head, and to keep her eyes shut very tight, but who could resist just a peek at the magic white clouds of steam rising from the luscious bowl of turkey stew, especially if the prayer had just begun the second quarter?

At last the baby, Pilgrim though she was, grew so hungry and so tired of the overlong prayer that she grasped the wooden spoon in her right hand and began to pound it up and down on the table, throwing her head back and her hands upward and exploding in sheer joy in her shrill little voice crying, "Whee, whee, whee."

The picture shows this very moment when the baby breaks into this grave and solemn prayer and interrupts the stern Pilgrim father's devotion by her exploding joy. The painter makes us laugh to see the long and awesome prayer breaking up under the force of the baby's uncontrollable spirit of joy. But I think the artist was doing something bigger than giving the passers-by in Bostontown just a chance to smile at the expense of the stern Pilgrim father. I think he was saying that there is more than one way to say a prayer of thanks. I think that he was saying that the baby with her radiant pink and white chubby face, with her tiny heart bursting with joy, and with her gleeful, "Whee, whee, whee," from her high chair was also saying to God, "Oh, thank you, thank you, thank you."

There are many ways of saying our prayers and sometimes the shortest prayers can come most directly from the heart. Jesus said that we are not heard for our much speaking nor for our long prayers. Isn't the best thanks we can give to God just to be "Thanks-living"? That means that every day and hour, we live as boys and girls who are so happy and grateful for our food, so glad for our homes, so grateful for our friends and our parents, so happy for our country and our church, that we are ready to burst with joy and exultant gladness of heart, remembering always that our heavenly Father is the giver of all these wondrously good and perfect gifts.

122

GRACE IN THE DINER

(*A Thanksgiving Sunday story*)

BILLY IS A WEE boy only three years old, but his eyes are so big and his round little red face is so jolly that whoever sees him wants to take him up and squeeze and kiss him.

All day long he seems happy and gay, and especially is he very polite. He never forgets to say, "Thank you," because he thinks it is right to be grateful.

Billy has his own special way of saying "thank you" to God. His mother taught him a thank-you prayer to say to God when he sits at the table before his dinner. But Billy does not think one prayer is thanks enough to God for his delicious breakfast or his nice dinner.

He likes to say "thank you" several times—not just once. So Billy bows his head over his orange juice at breakfast and repeats his "thank-you prayer" to God.

Later when his hot cereal comes, Billy sees that this is a beautiful new dish of delicious food to be grateful for, so he bows his head and says grace the second time.

Later still, when his mother serves him his steaming boiled egg, Billy bows his head to say the prayer of blessing for the egg. Three prayers of thanks for one breakfast!

One day Billy's mother took him for a long automobile ride, such a long ride that Billy said, "I'm hungry. I can't wait till I get home. I want to eat now."

The only place to get food along that road was a diner, an eating place built like a train-car where men sit up to the counter on high stools without taking off their hats.

Billy sat up on a high stool, too. That was fun.

When his soup was put in front of him, Billy bowed his head and said in his wee little voice:

> "God is great and God is good
> And we thank him for this food.
> By his hand must all be fed;
> Give us, Lord, our daily bread. Amen."

All the men who were sitting there jabbering and eating in a   123 hurry began to look around. Somebody was talking to God—of all things in a diner! Soon they spied Billy's little bowed head and looking very much surprised and ashamed they all stopped talking, took off their hats, and listened until Billy finished his prayer. Then they plopped their hats on their heads again and went back to eating with a rush.

After he had finished his soup, a plate of potato and meat was served to Billy. Billy bowed his head again and said in his wee little voice:

> "God is great and God is good
> And we thank him for this food.
> By his hand must all be fed;
> Give us, Lord, our daily bread. Amen."

The men stopped talking. This time they knew it must be Billy. They looked more surprised than ever, but they could not keep their hats on when a fine little boy was brave enough to say his prayers before strangers. Off came their hats and they listened until Billy had ended his "thank you" to God.

Once more the men plopped their hats back on their heads in a way that seemed to say. "I guess our food has had blessing enough for one meal." But they didn't know Billy.

Soon he was looking at a piece of blueberry pie with a big scoop of vanilla ice cream on top of it. Billy felt if ever he was grateful it was now. He bowed his head a little lower and said in his wee little voice:

> "God is great and God is good
> And we thank him for this food.
> By his hand must all be fed;
> Give us, Lord, our daily bread. Amen."

The men all looked at Billy a long time, then at each other as if to say, "What's going on here? Is this a prayer meeting?" But when they saw that Billy was very sincere and brave, they took off their hats a third time, and some of them even bowed their heads to join Billy in his prayer.

When Billy finished his dinner and got down off the stool, all the men came over to meet Billy, to shake him by the hand, and tell him how glad they were he came into the diner that day. Some of those men had long ago forgotten ever to say "thank you" to God.

Billy did not know what a fine sermon he had preached that day in the diner. He only thought he had said his prayer of thanks as everyone in the wide world should do to such a kind heavenly Father.

PRETZELS FOR PRAYERS

(Christmas)

A GOOD GERMAN PASTOR a long time ago said to his good wife— or at least this is the legend—"My dear, this is the happy Christmas season, and I would like to give something to each child in my church."

"But we are very poor," said the good wife, "and what can we afford to give all these many children?—Hans and Hilder and Wilhelm, Fritz, Gretchen, Hansel, and Frieda—oh, there are a hundred of them!"

"I know," said the pastor, "but you know, my good Frau, how much and how dearly I love every boy and girl in my church." He spoke like a good, true pastor should.

"Well now," said his Frau, "I will give you some of the money I have been saving—it's only a mite, but it may help."

The pastor kissed his wife's hand, "Thank you, thank you," he said. "Your mite will help mightily."

"I think I will give them each a stick of candy shaped and colored like ribbons."

"For shame," said his Frau, "you know candy is not good for children, and besides, when they are too poor even to have all the bread they need, why give them candy?" You see it was a very poor village and many children did not always have enough to eat.

"Then I will go to the baker and give them bread," answered the pastor, "but it shall be pretty bread that shall make them happy."

With that he took his wife's mite and his own mite, and pulling his hat down till it rested on his ears—you see it was an old hat— he trudged out the door, down the steps, and off to the baker's shop.

"Mister Baker," said the minister, "can you take some dough and make something pretty, something delicious, something *different* for the children of my church for a present?"

"Ach," said the jolly baker, as he bumped his stomach against the bread board. "It is for the children of your church, *vas est?"*

"Ya, ya," said the pastor, smiling broadly.

With that the baker took some dough in his hands and began to roll it into long, slender pieces like thin ropes. Then he twisted it into shapes of circles, triangles, towers, and trees.

"Ach, nein, nein," said the baker, "not so good—not pretty."

Then the baker pulled hard on his right ear and scratched his shiny bald head. "Let me tink," he said. "Do your children pray in the church?" asked the baker.

"Well, now," said the pastor, "would I be a good pastor if I did not teach the children to pray?"

"Ach, ya, ya. I remember now," said the baker. "When they pray you teach them to fold their hands like this. My Fritz does." (And here he crossed his right hand and his left hand on his arms.)

"Ya, ya," said the pastor, "I have taught them in my church to pray with their arms crossed like this."

A light gleamed in the baker's twinkly big eyes. He tossed a thin roll of dough in the air, caught it when it came down, and crossed the pieces of dough across a circle to imitate the arms of boys and girls in prayer.

"There," said the baker, "I will put a hundred of these in my oven and you may give them to remind your boys and girls always to say their prayers each night. I will make them a pretty, shiny brown. I will sprinkle them with a delicious salt, and they shall be crisp and chewy, and when the children eat them, they shall cry for more."

The pastor almost danced a jig he was so happy. "But what shall we call these?" he asked.

The baker grinned, "Why pretzels, of course—pretzels for prayers."

Special Day Stories

126

THE PREACHER WHO PLAYED BLIND MAN

(Christmas)

ONE DAY IN London a man stopped to talk on the street corner with a minister, the famous Dr. Dick Sheppard, who was pastor of the historic church with the tall tower in Trafalgar Square.

"Everyone is selfish and mean," complained the cynical citizen of London.

"Oh, but you are wrong; on the contrary, everyone is kind, very kind," answered the famous young preacher.

"You are twice wrong," retorted the man. "I know that everyone is selfish and mean, just like an old pig. It's every man for himself and the devil take the hindmost."

The young minister coughed with indignation. "I just know you're dead wrong," he said. "People are kind. But since you won't believe it, I shall prove it to you, and you shall eat your words." And with that, they both walked off in different directions.

Now the famous minister did a very strange thing. He put on an old, shabby coat, some dirty old shoes, took a cane, and put on a pair of dark, smoked glasses. With the dark glasses covering his eyes as if he were blind, he walked down the street to the Strand in London. No one could recognize him in this disguise.

When he came to the street corner, the people stopped their cars to let him get across safely. Sometimes a Boy Scout took his arm and helped him across the street; sometimes a man helped him. When he wanted to take a bus, the conductor got down off the seat and took his arm to help him up the steps into the bus. Some people even tried to put money into his hands.

"It was amazing," the minister told the boys and girls of his congregation afterwards, "how people made way for me everywhere and just surrounded me on all sides with kindness. I proved that people are kind by playing the part of a blind man."

It was a few days before Christmas when the minister met the man again on the street—the grouchy man who said that "everyone is selfish and mean like an old pig." Dr. Sheppard told the man what had happened.

Then he said, "Come with me into my study," and he led the man into his church.

127

Dr. Sheppard showed the man his desk stacked high with letters containing money sent by people all over the country who wanted to brighten the lives of the poor of London at Christmas. He led the man into another room in his church and showed him great baskets loaded with fruits, cakes, nuts, chickens, English plum pudding, cranberry sauce, pumpkin pie, candies, and many luscious things to eat given by people who wanted to be kind to the poor children. Then he led him through another door and showed him a big room crowded with toys, teddy bears, dolls, marbles, trains, toy fire engines, jackknives, balls, drums, horns, sleds, and mittens given by people who wanted to be kind to the poor at Christmas.

"Now," said the minister, looking squarely into the face of the man, "do you still say that everyone is mean and selfish just like an old pig?"

And true to his promise the minister made the man eat his words.

I think the good minister should have given this man his pair of dark, smoked glasses and should have said to him, "Here, you take these dark glasses and wear them, for if you can't see any kindness in people, not even at Christmastime, then you are a real blind man and you ought to wear a blind man's glasses."

THE UNWILLING STEWARD

(A stewardship story)

TED LOOKED at the bright new fifty-cent piece in his hands, and then smiled up at his father.

"Thanks for the allowance, Dad!"

"You've earned it, son," his father answered. "And by the way, don't forget to keep out your tenth for church."

A frown wrinkled Ted's forehead.

"Do I have to, Dad? If I keep on taking out a whole nickel every week, I'll never save enough for that catcher's mitt! Besides, Steve's father gives him extra money for church. He doesn't have to take it out of his allowance."

"Listen, son," Ted's father replied patiently. "We've talked about this before, remember? And we agreed that the whole idea of having an allowance in the first place was to learn how to use it—how to be a good steward."

"I know," Ted responded a bit gloomily. "But I don't see why boys like me have to be stewards. It's different with grown-up men. They're supposed to know how to use money, and besides, they have a lot more of it to start with. After all, when a fellow's just got fifty cents a week—"

"We have to prove we can be good stewards in little things before we're ready to tackle the big ones, son," his father replied. "You know, there's a verse in the Bible that says, 'Moreover, it is required of a steward that a man be found faithful.' It doesn't say faithful in big things —just faithful. So if you're faithful in putting aside that nickel every week—"

"All right, Dad," Ted sighed, as he slipped the money into his pocket. "I guess I'm a sort of unwilling steward."

Just then Ted's mother appeared in the doorway, all breathless and excited. "Ted, Mrs. Burton just phoned that she's been called to the hospital—her sister was in an accident—and Mr. Burton's out of town. She's already put Binky to bed, and there's no one to stay in the house. I can't go and leave Carol and Sue, and your father has a trustee's meeting at the church. So, Ted, you won't mind running over there for a while, will you?"

"Me—a baby-sitter?" Ted groaned. "What would Steve and the other fellows say if they ever knew I was out baby-sitting?"

"But this is an emergency, Ted," his mother argued.

"Of course Ted will help out," his father interrupted. "I'll drop him off on my way to church, and pick him up when the meeting's over. By that time Mrs. Burton should be home."

Ted followed his father out, pausing just long enough to say to his mother, "Promise you won't tell Steve!"

At the Burton's, Ted and his dad found their neighbor waiting at the door.

"Binky's fast asleep," she explained. "You can read or watch television or do whatever you like, Ted. I'll be back just as soon as I possibly can. I can't ever thank you enough for coming!"

Mrs. Barton flashed Ted a grateful smile and dashed out to her own car that stood waiting in the driveway.

"Good luck, Ted!" said his father, as he placed a reassuring hand on the boy's shoulder. "I'll be back in an hour or so."

129

"Sure thing, Dad. I'll manage," Ted answered, already feeling a little happier about his job. "See you later!"

Ted reached for a book on the library table. "Well, what do you know?" he grinned. "A dictionary! Exciting reading, that! But maybe I could look up that word 'steward' and see what old man Webster has to say about it.

"Here it is—'steward'—a supervisor, or manager. Mmm—that makes me a kind of steward tonight, I guess. After all, I'm the manager while Mrs. Burton's gone—supervising the house, and Binky and all. I'm a steward, that's what! A steward is much more dignified than a baby-sitter."

Suddenly Ted straightened up in his chair. Something was burning! He ran out into the kitchen. There was smoke puffing up the basement stairs. Ted reached for the light switch and made his way down the stairs. Mrs. Burton had left the iron plugged in, and the thick pad that covered the board was smoldering. Ted caught up a piece of clothing to protect his hands, yanked out the electric cord, and dashed to the laundry tubs. Several good dousings with cold water put out the slow flames, but what a mess the basement was! There was the floor to mop, the windows to open, then the first floor to air out. In the midst of all the work and confusion, Mrs. Burton returned.

"Ted!" she exclaimed. "Whatever is the matter? Is Binky all right?"

"Oh, yes," Ted answered comfortably. Ted was doing his best to reassure her when the doorbell rang and his father came in.

A short while later, when the Burton household was calm once more, Ted and his dad started home.

"You know, son," his father confided, "I'm proud of you."

"I was just being a good steward," Ted explained. "Oh, yes, and that reminds me, Dad, can you change fifty cents so I can get a nickel out for church?" He reached in his pocket and pulled out the shiny half dollar.

Somehow the catcher's mitt didn't seem too important now. Of course, he still wanted it, but it could wait a while. Ted knew that if he could be a good steward in one thing, like taking care of another person's property, he could be a good steward in others, too—things like giving back to God a part of what God had given him.

But what Ted did not know was this: Mrs. Burton was already on the telephone talking to his mother.

"I want to give Ted something to show my appreciation for what he did for me tonight," Mrs. Burton was saying. "Do you think he would like some baseball equipment, something like a catcher's mitt, for instance?"

—Adapted from a story by Mary Peacock, in *Juniors*.

THE STORY OF JOHNNY ROBIN

(For the first day of Spring)

JOHNNY ROBIN grew restless and discontented in his winter home in the marshland down in Florida. One day he cocked an eye at the sky and said, "I think I will fly north. Something inside me tells me that I will find springtime when I get up north in the Pocono Mountains of Pennsylvania."

All his young friends looked at him in excitement. Then Johnny said, "You know, I would like to be there on the first day of spring, just to sing to all the boys and girls as they go to school, 'Cheer up, cheer up, cheer up.' "

Some of the robins said, "Johnny, we want to fly with you, too." But others said, "Now don't be foolish, Johnny, it is much too early yet to go north," and then one old robin who was a joy-killer said that he knew for sure that spring would come much later this year.

"Yes," said Old Robin Grouch, "how do you know that spring might not decide to skip a year and never come at all this year?"

But all this did not discourage Johnny Robin. He was so sure he would find the springtime if he flew north that he stuck out his red breast and dandied up his gray coat, and spreading his wings with a yip, yip, yip, off he flew. Many robins flew with Johnny, but as the miles grew longer and longer, some

131

stopped to rest here and there while they journeyed along the way.

One day when Johnny was flying, he looked around and saw that he was flying all alone. But he was brave and did not mind for he said, "I want to be there in the Pocono Mountains on the first day of spring to sing to all the boys and girls on their way to school, 'Cheer up, cheer up, cheer up.'"

Johnny arrived at the Pocono Mountains just the very day before the first day of spring. But imagine how sad he was, for there was no springtime anywhere. The ground was all covered with snow and the icy wind blew and roared through the trees. Flakes of snow were falling on Johnny's wings and head as he flew through the air. Johnny saw no chance to get any dinner, except for a few crumbs which a good lady put in a little box on her window sill. Johnny was getting cold and soon he was shivering in every one of his little bones.

"Oh, dear, oh, dear," he said, "I must have made a mistake after all. I did come too far north and perhaps the springtime is skipping this year."

At last he found a little perch under a roof where he could get out of the chilling wind. There Johnny sat with his head hunched down into his feathers, wet and cold and discouraged, and with his tail drooping way down.

"Perhaps I should not have been so sure about the coming of spring," said Johnny, "and I certainly do not think I can sing to cheer up anybody." He was so chilled and sad and lonely that he would have cried himself to sleep, only robins cannot cry like we can.

Johnny Robin had come so far and was so very tired that he slept late the next morning. When he opened his eyes, he could hardly believe what he saw! A big yellow sun was flaming in crimson and shone all through the sky, and it was melting the snow away. The streams were running and singing a song with merry laughter. The green grass was appearing on the lawns. Johnny fluffed down his feathers, lifted up his head, flew down to the grass, and pulled up a fat worm for breakfast. Then over in a garden he saw yellow crocuses and purple ones, too. Just then Johnny flew up to the tippity-top branch of a pine tree, and expanding his little lungs to the limit, he sang his song, as the boys and girls went down the road to school, "Cheer up, cheer up, cheer up."

The boys and girls turned and pointed their fingers at him and they shouted, "It *must* be the first day of spring, for Johnny the Robin is here!"

Johnny Robin was so glad to see them, too. But what he did not know was that when they went to school, the teacher put his name upon the blackboard, for he was the very first robin anyone had seen that spring.

The Story of
Johnny Robin

hymn stories

DULL DAYS CAN BE FUN

(*For use with "America"*)

"WHAT CAN WE DO? There's no fun outdoors. It's a rainy day. It's just too dull with nothing to do." This is what Jim had moaned all day, lolli-gagging and moping around the house.

"Why, there are lots of interesting things to do," Jim's mother said, "if you just wake up and don't let a rainy day ruin all your plans."

"Did you ever hear of Benaiah or Sam Smith, and what they did on dull and dismal days?"

"No," said Jim. "Who is Benaiah? He sounds like a Bible name."

"He was," said Mother, "and he carried a name of glory and a place among the famous mighty men who were on the staff of King David."

"What did Benaiah do that was so wonderful?" asked Jim doubtfully.

"Well, he did many exploits—brave deeds in battle and in single-handed combat, but one of the reasons his name is on the roll of honor of David's thirty mighty men is because he did something on a dull day.

"One night a lion killed many sheep and goats, and the farmers asked David's soldiers to kill the lion who hid in a deep pit. That next morning it began to snow. The sky was dark and there was no sunlight. 'We can't see the lion in the pit on a dark, dull day,' said the soldiers and, therefore, they would not go out to kill the lion that day. 'Wait till the sun shines,' they said. But not Benaiah. He went out there in the whirly, whizzy snowstorm that almost blinded his eyes. He felt his way toward the pit. As he let himself down into the pit, he could hear the lion snarl and roar. He just walked into the lion's parlor where there were no lights and he killed that lion who had been eating the sheep. So ever after that men praised

Benaiah, because on a day that was snowy and dark and dull, 'he went down into a pit and slew a lion.' "

"Well, he was all right, I'll admit," said Jim, "but you also said something about Sam Smith."

"Oh, yes, well, Sam was a young man going to Andover Seminary to study to be a minister. It was a cold, snowy day that Sam called a dismal day—February in New England brings some shivery, raw, mean days and this was one of them. But like Benaiah, Sam Smith was determined that the bad day would not stop him from doing some mighty deed.

Sam Smith decided to look at some music and he found a tune that he liked—the tune had a perky punch and force. So Sam picked up a scrap of paper, never looking out-of-doors at the swirling gusts of blinding snow. Very quickly he wrote some verses of a song. On that dismal day in 1832 he wrote the song you all sing and know. More than 30,000,000 school children sing this song which was written by Rev. Samuel F. Smith:

> My country, 'tis of thee,
> Sweet land of liberty,
> Of thee I sing;
> Land where my fathers died,
> Land of the pilgrims' pride,
> From every mountain side
> Let freedom ring.

"After writing some stanzas young Sam Smith, who had graduated from Harvard with Oliver Wendell Holmes, wrote as the last stanza the following:

> Our fathers' God, to thee,
> Author of liberty,
> To thee we sing;
> Long may our land be bright
> With freedom's holy light;
> Protect us by thy might,
> Great God, our King."

When his mother finished, Jim was thinking hard. Suddenly he said, "I know something interesting I can do," and he was off with a bound as gay as a grasshopper.

Let us sing "America" this morning.

135

(For use with "Joyful, Joyful, We Adore Thee")

BOYS AND GIRLS, today we are going to sing a hymn of praise to God from our hymnbook, Number ___.

Now, if you will look at the top of the page, in the right-hand corner, you will see the name of the famous musician who composed the tune we will be singing. His name is Ludwig von Beethoven. You will see that this tune comes to us from the land of Germany.

Beethoven wrote nine famous symphonies. I am sure you have heard many of them played by great orchestras, perhaps in your symphony hall, or on the radio or on television, or you may have one of Beethoven's symphonies on your records at home.

This is how this tune was composed. One day Beethoven read a poem called "Ode to Joy" written by a famous German poet by the name of Schiller. This so inspired Beethoven that he wrote his "Ninth Symphony" from which is taken the tune of the hymn we will be singing.

Mr. Beethoven gave this music to the public audience for the first time over one hundred years ago in Vienna. He stood facing the orchestra with his baton and led the musicians in playing this great symphony of joy. Perhaps you remember that Beethoven himself was stone deaf and did not hear his own music while it was being played. Neither did he hear the people stamping, cheering, and whistling with delight because they were so excited with his wonderful music. The audience was in an uproar of joy. Beethoven, because he was facing the orchestra and was deaf, did not know what was happening until someone took him by the shoulder and turned him face about where he could see the excited audience. Now the people were standing, some on their seats, waving their arms and clapping, and many of them melting in tears because they recognized that Mr. Beethoven, himself, could not hear any of the wonderful music he had written.

The beautiful words of this hymn were written by Henry van Dyke, a teacher at Princeton University. He was staying in the Berkshire Hills in Massachusetts at Williams College when the words of this beautiful hymn came to him. He had just heard the music of Beethoven's Ninth Symphony. Van Dyke thought the music was so beautiful that it should be used as a hymn to sing in church.

As you sing this hymn today, remember that the words were written by an American, the music by a German, and that it is a song of great joy because all who love God are happy in their hearts.

THE MUSIC OF A LITTLE BLIND GIRL

(*For use with hymns by Fanny Crosby*)

HER PARENTS loved her dearly, she was such a bright baby. They were sure that they would be very proud of her, she was such a darling. She wiggled her little toes and tiny fingers and said, "Goo, goo," like all good babies do.

But as she began to grow older and to walk about, her eyes grew weak and tired until at last they could not see at all. Fanny Jane, for that was her name, could not see her father or her mother, her nurse, her teacher or playmates. She could not see her dog nor her pretty dresses nor her new shoes. She walked around as if it were always night. Her father and mother were very sad. They could not know that this little girl would make beautiful songs to sing and that her songs would be sung by boys and girls and men and women the world over.

In spite of being blind so young, Fanny Jane could never stand having people pity her. God helped her make up her mind that she would be a happy girl. When she was only eight years old she wrote,

> "To weep and sigh because I am blind
> I cannot, and I won't.
> Oh, what a happy soul am I
> Although I cannot see!"

Fanny Jane decided that if she could not see with her eyes, she could perhaps see things through her mind. She trained her keen mind to commit to memory many beautiful words in the Bible.

Then she learned to write poetry, even as a child. She wrote some hymns for the children of her Sunday school to sing.

She grew into a lovely young girl, and when she became a woman, everyone loved Fanny Jane Crosby, the famous blind writer of beautiful hymns.

137

Perhaps you have sung her hymns in our Sunday church school, and I am sure your parents have often sung many of her sweet songs. She wrote hundreds, even thousands, of poems that have been set to lovely music.

She showed her great love for Christ in one of her hymns:

> "Tell me the story of Jesus,
>   Write on my heart ev'ry word;
> Tell me the story most precious,
>   Sweetest that ever was heard.
> Tell how the angels, in chorus,
>   Sang as they welcomed His birth,
> 'Glory to God in the highest!
>   Peace and good tidings to earth.'"

Another hymn which many people love is the one she wrote which begins:

> "I am thine, O Lord, I have heard Thy voice,
>   And it told Thy love to me;
> But I long to rise in the arms of faith,
>   And be closer drawn to Thee.
> Draw me nearer, nearer, blessed Lord,
>   To the cross where Thou hast died;
> Draw me nearer, nearer, nearer, blessed Lord,
>   To Thy precious, bleeding side."

Perhaps you have sung, too, one of her best known hymns called, "Blessed Assurance, Jesus Is Mine!" You will remember the chorus:

> "This is my story, this is my song,
> Praising my Saviour all the day long;
> This is my story, this is my song,
> Praising my Saviour all the day long."

Yes, Fanny Jane Crosby was a happy, happy soul, because she loved God, even though she was blind. She saw many reasons to be thankful and to be always singing praise to God. One of her songs beautifully vibrates with her praise to God. Let us sing it this morning.

"Praise Him! praise Him! Jesus, our blessed Redeemer!
Sing, O Earth, His wonderful love proclaim!
Hail Him! hail Him! highest archangels in glory;
Strength and honor give to His holy name!
Like a shepherd, Jesus will guard His children,
In His arms He carries them all day long:
Praise Him! praise Him! tell of his excellent greatness;
Praise Him! praise Him! ever in joyful song!"

*The Music
of a Little
Blind Girl*

MOMO

MRS. E. L. ATKINS, who was a missionary to the black men of the Congo in Africa, told this story of something that happened to her one day.

"I was rolling pie crust on the table on the porch of my bungalow. Suddenly, I looked up and saw a giant African, with big muscles, crawling on his hands and knees up the steps to the porch of my bungalow.

"On his cheeks he had the cut marks of the tribe of the Bambalas. His teeth were filed, showing that he belonged to one of the cannibal tribes. He was naked except for a leopard skin loincloth and his black skin was shiny in the hot sun. Never before in his life had this black man of the deep forest seen a pair of steps, so, of course, he did not know that stairs were made to walk up on with the feet. That was why he was crawling up on his hands and knees on all fours as you probably did when you were a baby.

"At first I was alarmed. Then I said boldly in the native language, 'What do you want?' The African said, 'I want a string,' and made motions with his hands. Confused, I asked, 'What kind of string do you want?' The man with the black skin said, 'I want a string with red dots on it.' I was even more confused. 'What kind of string is that?' I asked. 'The string your husband wears around his neck,' he replied. So then I knew, of course, that what he really wanted was the necktie that my husband wore. I thought it wise to refuse his request. 'Oh, no, I cannot give away my husband's neckties!' I said. But then I thought that perhaps I could help this poor black man in some way if I would ask him to give me something in exchange for the necktie. So I said: 'I cannot give you a necktie of my husband's unless you give me a chicken.'

"Now he wanted the necktie badly. His eyes brightened; he smiled and showed his filed teeth. He went away running. After a long time he came back with the chicken. I gave him the necktie with the red dots. He was so delighted he jumped up and down like a little boy.

"Then I said, 'Tomorrow is our worship day here at the mission. Why don't you come and hear my husband, who wears these neckties, talk about a man called Jesus?'

"Sure enough the next day, which was Sunday, there was Momo of the cannibal tribe of the Bambalas sitting up on one of the front benches in the thatched roof church wearing his leopard skin loincloth and nothing else except my husband's necktie with the red dots around his neck. Of course, he had not known how to tie it properly. But oh! he paid such close attention while my husband preached about Jesus!

"The next day I was much surprised when Momo came again to our bungalow. He said, 'I want to ask you more about that man, Jesus. Your husband talked about him.' I said, 'If you want to know more about Jesus you must come to our school and learn to read. Then you can read a book which will tell you about Jesus. But you will have to go to school with boys who are much younger than you, only ten to twelve years old.'

"Momo was a grown man, strong and muscular, a great hunter, but he said he would sit in the class with the young boys because he was so eager to learn to read the book about Jesus. He came to school faithfully and learned to read the Bible because he wanted to go back to his tribe of Bambalas to tell them about Jesus. Then he asked to be sent to a more advanced school at Kimpesi where he could learn to be a preacher and an evangelist.

"So Momo finished his work at the seminary. Then he was ordained as a minister and became an evangelist, traveling from village to village holding services for boys and girls and men and women, telling them the wonderful story of Jesus.

"Momo, who first came climbing on his hands and feet up the stairs to my porch, has climbed a long way up the stairs that lead to God. Now he is a happy preacher of God's love to those who have never heard the story of that wonderful man called Jesus."

THE MOST FUN ISN'T MONEY

(A hospital in Haiti)

LARRY LIVED in Pittsburgh where his father was a multi-millionaire. With all that money in his family—"the Mellon Millions," people called it—Larry Mellon could have everything he wanted when he

142

was a boy—dogs, boats, ponies. Later in his teens he had riding horses, automobiles and a speed motorboat. He went to a rich man's college, but after one year he didn't go back to school. Perhaps he just wanted to be a playboy and have fun, for he had lots of money he could spend.

But one day something new and strange happened to Larry. He was looking through a picture magazine when he suddenly stopped turning the pages. There he read the story of a great musician, a famous organist, who had given up his fortune and his fame to go to Africa as a doctor. This man wanted to work as a medical missionary among the poor, sick black men who lived in the African jungles. The man's name was Dr. Albert Schweitzer.

"Why can't I do that, too?" Larry asked himself. He remembered that when he had traveled once to the West Indies he had seen the black women and children of Haiti covered with soil, and he saw that they were underfed and sick with disease. He had never quite forgotten what he saw. Now he remembered how sick and miserable they were.

"Why can't I become a doctor, too?" Larry asked himself again. "I can if I go back to school, and besides I've got the money to finish college, to learn how to become a doctor, and I can even build my own hospital for the poor people of Haiti."

So Larry went back to college for seven years. He graduated as a doctor with the skill and ability to help and heal sick people.

Then Larry did a very wonderful and unselfish thing. He took two million dollars of his own money and built in Haiti, in the midst of the poor, sick people, one of the finest hospitals in all the world. He built three operating rooms into his hospital. For that hot climate he made his hospital air-conditioned, and because there are sometimes earthquakes and cyclones in Haiti, he made his hospital earthquake-proof and cyclone-proof.

Now everyday the poor, sick women come to Dr. Larry and to his hospital to be cured. Dr. Larry Mellon has other nurses and doctors to help him.

"I am having the most fun I have ever had in my whole life," said Dr. Larry. "I know that to spend money isn't fun. I have learned that the most fun in life is not having money but helping others."

Then he points out the window at the front of his hospital. "But all this would never have happened but for that man out there." And there in front of this hospital, floodlighted at night beside a beautiful

143

fountain, is a statue of Dr. Albert Schweitzer, whose life as a medical missionary of Christ in Africa taught Larry the great joy of serving God by helping others.

THE SILENT BELL SPEAKS

(*A story about missions in China*)

WU CHANG and his sister Perfect Flower saw a crowd in the market place. A notice was posted on the wall of the village jail. Curiously the two Chinese children edged their way to the front of the crowd.

"Whoever shall possess any part of a Christian Bible from this day and thereafter," Wu Chang read, "shall be guilty of high crimes and shall be sentenced to a long jail term."

"And it's signed by Mayor Tuan himself," Perfect Flower gasped.

"Our fat, evil Mayor Tuan hopes to gain with the new government," said Wu Chang.

"Our new government is godless. They would be glad if we forgot all the Randolphs taught us about Jesus."

It had been almost three years since the American missionaries had had to leave their village. The mission house had been boarded up and a guard posted to make sure no one tried to enter it. Never since then had the mission church bell rung, calling the people to services.

But the children's father, the merchant Wu Lien, had still conducted secret meetings of the village Christians in the back of his shop.

Wu Chang entered his father's shop and told him about the mayor's decree.

That very night two of Mayor Tuan's soldiers burst into their house in the middle of the night and dragged Wu Lien out of bed. They took him off to jail, because they had found a Christian Bible in his room.

The next evening was the regular night for the prayer meeting in the back of Wu Lien's shop. Wu Chang was going to conduct the meeting in his father's absence.

"I am glad to see so many here in spite of the mayor's decree," Wu Chang said. "I am sure you will make protests when you hear that my father has been unjustly imprisoned because he possessed a Christian Bible."

144

There were murmurs of sympathy for Wu Lien, but it was clear the villagers were frightened and would not help.

"It will take a miracle, a ringing of a tongueless bell, to help us," a wrinkled old woman declared. This was an old Chinese expression for a miracle.

The next morning Wu Chang went to the metal worker's shop where bells were made.

"Do you know why the mission church bell does not ring even when the wind moves it?" he asked Fang, the metal worker.

"The tongue was taken out of the mission bell so it would not ring," he answered.

Wu Chang told Perfect Flower what he intended to do. The next day he went by the mission with some brass tongs hidden under his clothing. The guard told him to move on. Then the guard sat down on the mission steps to take a nap in the afternoon sun.

Wu Chang walked around in back of the mission and found a boarded-up window. He had to work quickly. He pried away the boards. He found the stairway to the cupola where the bell was. Then, after climbing the stairs, he began striking the bell with the brass tongs. It made a magnificent noise.

In a few minutes Wu Chang heard the guard breaking into the building and running up the stairs. "Stop that, you evil boy!" he shouted, dragging Wu Chang from the bell.

But it was too late. Already the Christian people were streaming from their houses. Many had their Bibles or New Testaments in their hands. For three years the bell had been silent. This was surely a miracle!

"The tongueless bell speaks," one Christian neighbor declared to the next. "The tongueless bell speaks for Jesus!"

Up the hill to the mission the people walked.

Mayor Tuan had recognized the sound of the bell. He had gone to the mission to see what had happened to make the bell ring. Now he was shaking his fat fist at Wu Chang. "You will suffer the same fate as your father for this!" Mayor Tuan shouted.

The crowd had reached the mission now.

"You must arrest the others, too," Wu Chang told the mayor. "Many have Bibles or New Testaments."

"But the jail is not big enough to hold all of them," the mayor protested. "Besides if all these people are in jail, how will I collect enough taxes to pay my salary?"

145

The crowd stirred uneasily. They were waiting for what the mayor would do now.

"Very well," Mayor Tuan fumed, stamping his foot. "You may keep your Bibles!"

"What of Wu Lien?" some brave person asked. "Are you going to keep him in jail for something that is no longer a crime?"

"Very well, Wu Lien will go free," said the mayor, stamping his foot again.

That night Wu Lien and his children were reunited. "Every night I prayed that God would help me, as Jesus had taught me to believe," he said. "And with Wu Chang's help, he did!"

—Adapted from a story by
Morton Green, in *Juniors.*

stories of our presidents

REMEMBER THE OFFERING
(*Calvin Coolidge*)

SOMETHING STRANGE happened in church one Sunday, and the pastor saw what happened. Now, he was the President's pastor and he could not help but see what was going on down there in the pew where the President of the United States sat with his wife and his two teenage boys. What the pastor saw he told a friend who told me, and now I am telling you. It happened this way.

Mr. Calvin Coolidge, one of our Presidents, had two sons, John and Calvin, Jr. They sat with their father and Mrs. Coolidge in the family pew up near the front of the church. You see, our Presidents, being wise men, do not try to sit in the way-back seats, for they like to be up front to see everything—the way we do at basketball games.

The Coolidge family attended the First Congregational Church in Washington, our nation's capital. Their pastor's name was Dr. Jason Noble Pierce.

President Coolidge was a good father who carefully taught his boys (they were about twelve and fourteen years old) to be quiet and reverent in church and to try to listen to the sermon. And Mr. Coolidge also had taught his sons to give an offering each Sunday out of their weekly allowance. Mr. Coolidge, like all good church fathers, wanted John and Calvin to remember that all we have comes from God our Father. He wanted the boys always to say "Thank you" to God by giving some of their own money and placing it on the offering plate.

But one Sunday when the offering was being taken a strange thing happened. The usher standing at the pew handed the offering plate to the President, who always sat at the end of the pew next to the aisle. Mr. Coolidge first put his offering on the plate, then Mrs. Coolidge put her offering on the plate. John put his offering on the plate, but Calvin, Jr. did not put his offering on the plate. The plate

147

was passed back to the usher in the aisle who went to the other pews, and after finishing taking the offering joined the other ushers at the back of the church.

Why did Calvin, Jr. not put his offering on the plate? Did he forget it? Did he think his father did not see him holding back? Did he want to keep the money to spend for something he wanted for himself? Or did he just decide he did not feel like saying "Thank you" to God that morning? Well, no one knows. But this is not the end of the story.

All the ushers in the church had finished taking up the offering through the pews and had joined together in a group, marching down the center aisle of the sanctuary to the front of the church. When they reached the President's pew, Mr. Coolidge leaned over the edge of the pew and touched the elbow of the usher next to him. The usher stopped, surprised, wondering what could be wrong.

"Please give me the offering plate," said the President in a low whisper. The usher handed the plate to the President. Everyone in the church was now wondering what could be happening. What did they see?

They saw Mr. Coolidge pass the plate down the pew to his boy who was holding back his money. In a low, soft voice the President said, "Son, your offering please." Blushing and with a quick motion the boy reached into his pocket and took out his offering and put it on the plate. During the hush in the church, Mr. Coolidge returned the plate to the usher, and the ushers then continued their march down the aisle to receive the prayer of blessing over the offering.

"Well, there's one father," the people in the church nodded, "who wants his boy to learn always to say 'thank you' to God and never to refuse to give his offering in church." And you may be sure that young Calvin never held back his offering again.

THE COLLEGE BOY AND THE MUSICIAN

(Herbert Hoover)

SOMEDAY YOU may go to college like Herb and Bill who were friends attending a college in California called Stanford University. These two boys did not have much money, and so they had to struggle to earn their way through college. They had to think how they could earn hundreds of dollars to pay their college bills. Fortunately they were full of bright ideas.

One day Herb, who was reading the newspaper, looked up and said to Bill, "Oh, Bill, I know a way out of our trouble. I know how we can earn loads of money. The world's greatest piano player is going to visit America. His name is Paderewski, and he comes from Poland. Let us ask him to come here and we will have a great concert. Everyone wants to hear Paderewski play the piano, he is so marvelous."

Bill jumped up from his chair, slapped Herb on the back, and said, "Marvelous, I am with you!" They ran to the Western Union and sent a wire to the master musician. He agreed to come and play, but the price he charged was very big—$1,600 for the one night. The two boys dashed around and hired a big hall, had tickets printed and flaming posters made, inviting everyone to come to the concert and buy a ticket. It was the biggest thing the two boys ever had tried to do together. They did well, but not as well as they had expected.

When the great concert was over and they had counted how much money they had taken in and how much money they had left after paying for the posters, tickets, and hall they had rented, they had only $1,200 left. They needed $400 more to make good their promise to pay Mr. Paderewski the $1,600. They were beside themselves with fear. "What shall we do?" they asked each other.

Bill said, "They say these great musicians demand their rights."

"I hope we don't get put in jail for not paying our bills," said Herb. "I'll tell you what we will do. We will write out a promise on a piece of paper that we will pay $400 more to Mr. Paderewski as soon as we can earn the money."

"Yes," said Bill, "but how are we going to earn that money?"

The two boys went to the room at the back of the stage trembling and afraid. They frankly told Mr. Paderewski they were $400 short. They paid him $1,200 and then handed him the paper with the promise to pay $400 more. How surprised they were when Mr. Paderewski smilingly tore up the promise to pay $400 more, and said, "That is all right, boys. I know you are trying to earn your way through college, and you just forget that $400." But they were even more surprised when Mr. Paderewski counted out $600 from the $1,200 they had given him and said, "Here, boys, you need this money more than I do. I want you to take $600 to help you pay your way

The College Boy and the Musician

149

through college." Herb and Bill had never dreamed that the great musician was such a sensitive, kind man. They had only thought he was a great musician.

Many, many years went by and they only heard of Mr. Paderewski through the newspapers. They learned that the great musician had become a great statesman and was now the Prime Minister of Poland. Herb became a famous man, too, and when a great world war broke over the nations, he was made American Relief Administrator to ship wheat and other food to the poor, starving people of Europe. Herb got word that the people of Poland were hungry and starving in a great famine, with their children crying for bread. So Mr. Herbert Hoover, for that was Herb's real name, sent big shiploads of wheat to Poland.

Now to whom do you suppose he addressed the wheat? To the Prime Minister, of course, Mr. Paderewski! Herbert Hoover had not forgotten how Paderewski had helped him when he was a college student at Stanford University. Now he had a chance to help Mr. Paderewski and all his starving friends. Even then, Mr. Paderewski hadn't the faintest idea that he had ever met or known Mr. Herbert Hoover.

One day, Mr. Hoover flew over to Paris. When Mr. Paderewski heard this, he flew down to Paris to thank Mr. Hoover for saving the people of Poland from starvation. Now it was Mr. Paderewski's turn to be surprised. Mr. Hoover shook hands with him warmly and said, "You don't remember me, but I have never forgotten you and your kindness. I was just a stranger to you—a college boy in California, but that $1,000 you gave us back that night after the concert many years ago helped me to remember always to be kind to other people."

"A LITTLE PRAYER OF MY OWN"

(Dwight Eisenhower)

"Now, DAN," said Dad, "don't forget to say your prayers before you hop into bed."

Dan turned suddenly around and looked at his father. "Do I have to say a prayer of my own? I have been to Sunday school and church today. I heard the minister pray and our teacher pray and we all joined in the Lord's Prayer. Why do I have to say a prayer of my own?"

"That is a good question," said Dad, "and I am glad you asked it. Let me tell you, Dan, what happened when I was down in Washington, our nation's capital.

"Crowds were pouring off the trains and the streets were jammed with automobiles. People from every state in the United States were coming to the grounds around the Capitol. People came from foreign countries, too—ambassadors and diplomats, some of them dressed in colorful uniforms. Of course there was a huge parade of men from the Army, the Navy, the Marine Corps, and the Air Force, and high overhead great swarms of jet planes were roaring across the sky.

"You see, these thousands of people had come to see the great event known as Inauguration Day. That is the day when the man who has been elected the President of these great United States stands on a platform on the steps of the Capitol and raises his hand above the open Bible, and makes a solemn promise to be a good President and serve the people with all his strength and ability. Of course, there were many people on the platform and the crowds were waiting for the President to arrive.

"The President knew that this was a great and solemn duty he was beginning and, so, early that morning, he had gone to church. He had listened to his own pastor as he prayed for him that God would give him strength and enable him to serve our country. Then he drove in an automobile amid the cheers that echoed and reechoed along Pennsylvania Avenue until he ascended the platform on the steps of the Capitol, astounded by the thunderous applause of the tens of thousands of Americans who loved him. The great and famous bishop came forward to offer prayer for this President and to ask God's blessing upon our nation, and then the President raised his hand above the Bible and took the pledge to be true to America and to God.

"Now, Dan, the President had been to church that morning. He had listened to a prayer by the famous bishop, and he had made a great promise over the open Bible and yet, Dan, do you know what he said when he got up to speak? This is what Dwight Eisenhower said: 'And now, if you will pardon me, I have *a little prayer of my own* that I would like to read to you.' This is the prayer of his own which he offered:

151

" 'Almighty God, as we stand here at this moment we beseech that thou make full and complete our dedication to the service of the people of this throng and their fellow citizens everywhere.

" 'Give us, we pray, the power to discern clearly right from wrong, and allow all our words and actions to be governed thereby and by the laws of this land.

" 'Especially we pray that our concern shall be for all the people, regardless of station, race, or calling. May co-operation be permitted and be the mutual aim of those who, under the concept of our Constitution, hold to differing political belief so that all may work for the good of our beloved country, and for thy glory. . . . Amen.'

"You see, Dan, the bigger the man is, the more often he feels the need of prayer. If the President of the United States, after hearing all the other prayers, felt that he needed a little prayer of his own, I imagine you will have a little prayer of your own, too, Dan. What do you think?"

SEASICK ASHORE

(Abraham Lincoln)

IN THE PRESIDENT'S office at the White House in Washington, there was the sound of a loud crash. People rushed into the room, and there lay the President, Abraham Lincoln, stretched out full length upon the floor.

"What has happened?" they asked. "Is the President dead?"

"No," said his helpers. "Mr. Lincoln has just fainted."

"But what made him faint?" the people asked.

Then they turned toward a man standing in the room, and someone pointed his finger at him and said, "That man came in here very angry, shaking his fists at Mr. Lincoln, and shouting in a mad voice, 'You must stop giving an order that we cannot shoot and kill the soldiers who deserted from the Army. You must not protect these cowards. We want to kill them, and you are too kindhearted.'

"The kindhearted President jumped up shaking his fists at the angry man and shouted back, 'If you think that I, of my own free will, will shed another drop of blood of another soldier. . . .' " But President

Lincoln never finished that sentence. At that moment he fell with a crash to the floor in a dead faint.

Now the doctors had rushed in and they were leaning down over his stricken body, listening to his heart, and holding his wrist, feeling his pulse.

"This terrible war," the doctors said, "is slowly killing the President. He must be put to bed immediately for a rest, and then he must go away from Washington and from his office in the White House for a complete change."

So, a few days later, President Lincoln went for a cruise on the big boat called *The River Queen.* It was early springtime, in the month of March. The river was wide and rough. The March wind was blowing hard, kicking up huge waves. *The River Queen* rocked from side to side and lurched forward and backward like a rocking horse. The President, who was already feeling badly enough, now began to feel seasick.

As the boat arrived at the wharf and the sailors tied the rope to make the boat fast to the dock, General Grant came up the gangplank to greet the President. He was followed by his staff of Army officers all resplendent in their dark blue uniforms trimmed with gold braid and brass buttons.

President Lincoln put out his long arm and gave all the officers a warm handshake. But they could see that he was really feeling very sick indeed.

"I am not feeling well today," Mr. Lincoln said to one of the officers. "As you can see, it was terribly rough coming down the bay, and I am well shaken up with seasickness."

Just then a young officer came up, who thought he could help President Lincoln to feel better. Out from his pocket he drew a bottle of champagne. He held the bottle up to Mr. Lincoln saying, "Drink this and it will cure you of your seasickness."

Now if this young officer had only remembered what a wise man President Lincoln was, he never would have offered him that strong drink.

Mr. Lincoln frowned as he put his hand on the young officer's shoulder, "No, no, no, my young friend," he replied. "I cannot take your drink. I have seen too many men in my day taken sick from drinking just what you have in that bottle. That strong drink makes them seasick ashore."

President Lincoln knew that it was bad enough to be seasick on   153

the water without being also seasick on the land. He knew how drinking liquor made one's legs all wobbly and twisted up with each other. It made one's head so dizzy a person could not see straight. He sometimes bumped into posts or sometimes fell into the gutter. It made one just as sick as if he were out on a stormy ocean. When men are drunk the solid land looks as though it were rising and falling and twisting like a ship in a tempest at sea.

"No, no, no," said one of America's greatest Presidents. "Don't touch any liquor. It will make you seasick ashore!"

And some day, when all America comes to know how wise President Lincoln was, and follows his example, no one will ever be so silly as to drink liquor and get seasick ashore.

154

SOCKS FOR THE PRESIDENT

IN THE SPRING of 1857, a little over one hundred years ago, a very strange expedition was starting out from Texas for California. It was a herd of seventy camels which had been brought from Arabia. Major Wayne of the United States Army wanted to find out if camels might not be useful in helping to open up America's own great desert in the Southwest.

And now Pauline Shirkey was riding on the back of a big, bumpy-backed dromedary, and she seemed to bob in all four directions at once as the funny animal lifted and plunked down each big, soft foot in turn.

"Barrak!" shouted Hadji Ali. This was the command for the camel to lie down.

"But camels walk so slowly," said Pauline's cousin, John. "It will take them ever so long to reach Los Angeles. I should think horses would be much better."

Hadji Ali shook his turbaned head. "No, my young friend. This lesson you Americans have yet to learn. In the desert it is not speed, but persistence, which finishes the journey. Camels keep going when horses give up. Camels eat thistles and cactus and live without water, when horses would die of starvation and thirst."

Just then Pauline's mother called. "It's time for your knitting lesson. You're ready to turn the heel of the sock you are making for Grandpa. Watch me carefully. Then you may try a few stitches yourself."

Pauline sighed. It was so much more fun riding a camel than counting, "Knit two, purl two." It was fortunate that Grandpa wasn't depending on Pauline for the pair of socks. She had started them for his Christmas gift last year, and now it was June.

The next morning Hadji Ali picked up a handful of camel's hair and dropped it in Pauline's lap. "Camels shed just like kittens," he said. "In my country, young ladies like you weave fine cloth from camel's hair."

"Couldn't camel's hair be knitted into socks and such things?" asked John. And the Major nodded.

155

"You can knit, Pauline," said the Major. "And your mother brought her spinning wheel all the way from Virginia. Why don't you try something that never has been attempted before. I shall want to see the results of your experiment, Pauline."

Snorting and complaining, the herd of camels started for San Antonio, the first stop on their westward journey. The children watched until the tinkle of the camel bells could no longer be heard. Then Pauline turned to her cousin John and said, "Now see what you got me in for! You know very well how I hate knitting!"

Mrs. Shirkey showed the children how to spin the camel's hair into yarn. "I'm not sure how thick to make it," she said. "Knitting socks from camel's hair is as new to me as sending camels to California."

"Knit two, purl two." Pauline was counting again. "Oh, dear," she sighed. "Something is wrong. I must have dropped a stitch somewhere. I'm afraid only a camel could wear this funny sock I'm making."

Her mother came to look. She felt the thickness between her fingers and shook her head. "We made the yarn too coarse. We'll have to spin it finer and try again."

"But, Mother, why do we have to go to so much trouble? Wool yarn is all right, and we have lots of that."

"But you promised to make the socks of camel's hair," said her mother.

So back to the spinning wheel they went, and Pauline pulled and twisted yarn much finer this time. Then back to the knitting needles. Knit two, purl two, rip out stitches, try again.

One day a letter came from Major Wayne. He said the camels had kept going patiently and persistently, despite many hardships. He was sure that in the end they would reach Los Angeles safely.

"Wouldn't it be fun to have a pair of camel's hair socks waiting for him when he gets there?" suggested Mother.

"We could send them by fast, cross-country stage," Cousin John added.

So Pauline picked up her knitting needles again and worked along, slowly at first, then faster and faster, as she became more expert. At last the two socks were finished and on their way to Major Wayne.

Weeks passed and then a letter came from California. It was addressed to Pauline.

"My dear young friend:

Imagine my surprise and delight, at the end of my journey, to find a fine pair of genuine camel's hair socks in the post for me. They prove that you have the same determination that has brought my helpers and our patient beasts through mountains and deserts to our destination. I shall have much to include in my report to President Pierce. Your grateful friend,

MAJOR WAYNE"

Socks for the President

More weeks passed. The camel's hair socks were almost forgotten. Then one chilly autumn morning, the big iron knocker on the plantation house door pounded importantly. Pauline's cousin John opened the door. A messenger handed him a small, square package.

"It's from Washington!" John shouted. "And it bears the official seal of the President of the United States!"

Mrs. Shirkey examined the package. "There must be some mistake," she said. But no. The label and the address were quite correct.

"Open it! Open it!" the children shouted. Off came the wrappings, off came the lid of the cardboard box. Inside they found a beautiful silver goblet. On its side was engraved the name of Franklin Pierce, fourteenth President of the United States.

A note in the package explained that this was in appreciation of the gift of the first pair of camel's hair socks ever made in America. Major Wayne had sent them on with his report to the President.

"Little did I think I was making socks for the President!" gasped Pauline.

The Civil War ended the experiment and camels were never used again for transportation in America. But long after they were forgotten, a pretty silver goblet and a note from the President reminded Pauline of the day when she had tackled a difficult task and had seen it through.

—Adapted from a story by Seth Harmon, in *Juniors*.

prayers

PASTORAL PRAYERS FOR CHILDREN

THE BUSY PASTOR may often call the children to the front of the church and there offer a prayer with the children grouped around him. He may do this instead of telling a story. Below are a few simple prayers which may be helpful and suggestive.

JESUS AS A CHILD

O GOD, our heavenly Father, we thank you that Jesus was once a child and that he played with other children and went to church on God's holy day. We thank you that he was obedient to his parents and that he loved the place of prayer where we worship you. Help us to know that because he was a child, he is very near us today. He enters into all our joy and play and into all our gladness of worship. For Christ's sake, we pray. Amen.

JESUS AS A BOY

O GOD, our heavenly Father, we thank you that Jesus was once a boy and that he played with other boys and girls and went to church on God's holy day. We thank you that he was obedient to his parents and that he loved to go to the place where people prayed and worshiped God. Help us to know that because Jesus was a child, he is very near to all boys and girls today. He enters into all our joy and play and into our gladness of worship. Bless us, we pray, in Jesus' name. Amen.

JESUS GREW

O GOD, we thank you that Jesus grew as a boy in wisdom and in stature and in favor with God and man. We thank you that he was always kind and helpful and a friend to everyone.

158   We are so glad that he is our best Friend, and that he likes to

have us happy, and he likes to have us pray to God. We thank you that he wants us to do the right and to be kind, and that he has promised to help us when we are in need. May we grow up to be more like him, always good and kind and strong. In Jesus' name, we pray. Amen.

JESUS OUR BEST FRIEND

O GOD, we thank you that Jesus once was small and grew in strength and in wisdom and in favor with God and man. We thank you that he was always kind and helpful and a friend to everyone.

We thank you that he is our best Friend, and that he likes to have us laugh, and that he likes to have us pray. We thank you that he likes us to be good and kind and that he has promised to help us whenever we are in any need. Grant that we may grow like him to be good and kind and strong and a friend to everyone who needs us. In Jesus' name, we pray. Amen.

JESUS AND THE BOY'S GIFT

DEAR GOD, our heavenly Father, we thank you for these quiet moments when we can bow our heads and talk with you. We thank you that Jesus invited the boys and girls to come to him and took them up in his arms and blessed them. So we know today that he welcomes us and wants us to come.

We thank you for the boy who gave him his lunch of loaves and fishes, because he, too, wanted to help. We thank you for blessing that small gift. We thank you today that you are glad whenever we do something for you. For your holy name's sake. Amen.

THANKS FOR MANY THINGS

O GOD, we thank you for giving us so many lovely things to enjoy. We thank you for our playground, for the boys and girls in our school and in our Sunday school. We thank you for our beautiful church and for all our friends in church. We thank you that it is a place we love to come to because we have such happy times here.

Will you help us to grow up always to love and serve you with our might and our minds and all our hearts?

Bless the children who do not know you and those who live in countries where they do not have all the many things to enjoy that we have. May we, in our giving, help them to know about Jesus and to be happier for Jesus' sake. Amen.

159

HELPERS IN THE CHURCH

WE THANK you this morning, our Father, for all the helpers in our church—the choir and the organist, the ushers, the deacons (the elders), and the trustees. We thank you for our Sunday school teachers, our janitor, and the one who arranges the flowers which remind us of all your beautiful gifts. We thank you for the Bible, and our hymnbooks, our Sunday school books and papers. Help us to be glad that we know your church. For Jesus' sake, we pray. Amen.

THANKS FOR SCHOOL

KIND HEAVENLY Father, we thank you for school days and our chance to learn so many wonderful things about your wonderful world. We thank you for our teachers who help us learn each day about the great and wondrous things that you have made. Help us to like our school and our books so that we may grow in wisdom and in stature.

We want to thank you, too, for the bus drivers and the policemen who help us get safely to school. Help us to be kind as Jesus would be to all the boys and girls in our school. In his name, we pray. Amen.

PARENTS

O GOD, our Father, we thank you for our fathers and mothers who brought us to the church this morning. We thank you that we can sit together as a family in the pew with our brothers and sisters, our parents, and our friends, singing and praying together as one family of God. Help our parents to know how much we do love them. Dear Father, take care of them that they may always be well and strong and happy in our homes.

Forgive us when we have been unkind to our parents or said or done disobedient things. Help us to love each other very dearly. For Jesus' sake, we pray. Amen.

THANKS FOR MANY THINGS

DEAR GOD, we thank you this beautiful morning that you want us to talk with you. We come to thank you that you made us so happy and gave us so many wonderful things to enjoy in our beautiful world.

We thank you for our parents, for our teachers, our Sunday school and our church. We thank you for our playmates and our friends. We thank you for America, our homeland, but most of all we thank you for Jesus Christ, our wonderful Friend and Savior.

Help us to love him more each day. May we try harder to please
him and to grow to be like him. In Jesus' name, we pray. Amen.

NOT TO BE AFRAID

O GOD, whose Son Jesus was not afraid of the cross and its suffering,
help us to be brave and to have courage. May we put our trust in
thee, our Almighty Father. Thou art strong to save and to keep us.
May we never fear, knowing that thy strong arms are around us. In
Jesus' name, we pray. Amen.

WHEN WE ARE SORRY

DEAR GOD, we do love thee very much. We are humbly sorry that
we have ever done wrong. Cleanse our hearts and make pure our
thoughts. May we love thee more truly and follow thee more closely
in all our work and play. Help us to walk in the footsteps of Jesus
and to copy his example. Amen.

FOR THE SICK

O GOD, we thank thee for mothers and doctors and nurses and our
hospitals. Bless all today who are helping those who are sick to get
well as Jesus did. Bless and heal our friends _____ and
_____ and _____. May they soon be with us
again, well and strong and happy. In Jesus' name, we pray. Amen.

DOING RIGHT

OUR FATHER God, we thank thee for our home, our church, and
our friends. Help us to do right even when it is hard. Make us
strong against cheating or lying that we may speak always the truth
with kindness. Help us to be fair in our play and obedient to our
parents. For Jesus' sake, we pray. Amen.

FORGIVENESS

O GOD, our kind Father, who lovest us so much, we thank thee
that thou didst send thy Son, Jesus, to live and to die for us. In our
Savior's name we ask thee to forgive us for any wrong we have
done and to pardon all our mistakes. Make us strong and glad to
do right. Amen.

THE GIFT OF OUR BODIES

O GOD, we thank thee for health and strength and our young bodies which can run and climb and jump and play in many games. We thank thee for our eyes that see so many beautiful things thou hast made. We bless thee for our ears which can hear music in church, the singing of the birds, and the voices of our playmates calling to us. We thank thee for our hands which can feel, and our voices which can sing songs of praise to thee. Thank you, dear God, for these gifts. Amen.

A MORNING PRAYER

WE THANK thee, our kind Father in heaven, for keeping us safely through all the dark hours of the night and for waking us fresh and happy from our sleep to this bright morning.

We thank thee for our church, our home, and our friends. Help us never to hate anyone and to forgive those who have not been kind to us. Forgive us if we have quarreled, and forgive us for all the many wrong things we have done. Make our hearts kind with love that we may not be jealous of others or dislike them. Make us more like Jesus. In his name, we pray. Amen.

MORNING PRAYER OF PRAISE

O GOD, our heavenly Father, we thank you that we are meeting this morning in your house. We are happy for all the wonderful things you have made. We are glad, too, because we know you have made us and will care for us. Be with us through all the hours of this holy day and go with us to our homes and to our school throughout the coming week. In the name of Jesus, our best Friend and Savior, we pray. Amen.

MORNING PRAYER

O GOD, we thank thee for this springtime morning as beautiful as fresh flowers. We thank thee for the gay, brilliant colors the flowers are wearing—the daffodils, the tulips, the violets and the crocuses. We thank thee for the warmth of the friendly sun kissing the flowers in the gardens and the fields. We thank thee that soon the buttercups, the daisies and the poppies will unfold their colors. We thank you that Jesus loved the flowers, too. Make us as beautiful and as fragrant in our lives as the spring flowers. In Jesus' name, we pray. Amen.

JESUS AND NATURE

O BLESSED GOD, who sent us Jesus, the Friend of boys and girls, we thank you for this beautiful springtime morning. We thank you that Jesus loved the brooks and the birds and the flowers of the field just as we do. We thank you that he took notice even of the sparrows and of the hens and of the chickens.

We thank you that Jesus knows and understands us and loves the things that we love and wants us always to love God, his heavenly Father and ours. Help us to be glad that he calls us to be his friends and to follow him. In his name we pray. Amen.

THE RAINY SUNDAY

OUR FATHER, we thank you for the showers of rain today which water the thirsty flowers. We thank you for the raindrops which help to make the grass so soft and green. We thank you that the brooks run with laughter on their way to the great rivers that run to the sea. Help us to love the sunshine all the more because we have walked in the rain. For Jesus' sake, we pray. Amen.

CHRISTMAS

O GOD, our Father, we thank thee that the angels sang when Jesus was born in Bethlehem. We thank thee that a bright star shed its light to guide the wise men through the night to the stable where the baby lay. We thank thee for the joy and gladness and singing which fill our lives at Christmas time. We thank thee for stockings hanging by our fireplace and the lighted candles in our windows and for the Christmas tree in our living room. We thank thee for the lovely gifts we receive. But at this holy Christmas time, dear God, we want to give the gift of our lives to thee in loving loyalty and worship. In the name of the Babe of Bethlehem, we pray. Amen.

SEASONAL PRAYERS FOR CHILDREN

IN AUTUMN

(Let the pastor hold in his hand a few brilliantly colored twigs of fall foliage, such as maple, oak, birch, or aspen. After the prayer let

163

him give the bright branches to the juniors to take to their department in the Sunday church school.)

Prayers

O GOD, the Infinite Artist, our heavenly Father, we are glad for the reds, yellows, and the browns, and all the bright colors you have printed the leaves of our trees this fall season. We thank you that you created them, because you love many colors, too. We thank you for the many patterns and designs of the different leaves. We are glad that the trees seem so gay and joyous, as if they were clapping their hands with gladness in praise of the heavenly Father. We praise you for all your wonderful kindness and your good gifts to us, and especially for the friendly fall leaves and their beautiful dresses. In Jesus' name, we pray. Amen.

IN WINTER

(In winter when branches of trees are bare, a pastor may hold in his hand branches of evergreen trees, cedars, pines, fir, hemlock, and so forth. After the prayer he may give the branches to the juniors to carry to their rooms in the Sunday church school.)

O GOD, we thank you for the friendly trees that stay green all through the winter days and the long year. When other leaves fade and drop to the ground leaving only bare branches, we thank you for the trees which still keep their branches always green. We are glad for the smell of the cedars, the perfume of the pines, and the firs which give us Christmas trees to make us happy.

Help us to be your friends everyday and everywhere all the year. May we keep our young lives true and beautiful in summer and winter, in springtime and in autumn, and serve you everyday of the year like the evergreen trees. In Jesus' name, we pray. Amen.

AFTER A SNOWSTORM

O GOD, our Father, we thank you that you are the Beautiful Artist who sent us the soft, white snow last night. We thank you for the many, many designs of the tiny snowflakes so beautifully formed. We are glad you take so much pains to make even one tiny snowflake a beautiful pattern. We are glad for all the fun the snow brings to us boys and girls: skiing, sliding, making snowballs, and building snowmen. Help us never to throw hard snowballs to hurt someone or to cause injury or damage of any kind. May we enjoy the snow as

164

your gift and always help others to enjoy it, too. O thank you, God, for your wonderful gifts to us. Thank you most of all for Jesus and help us to be like him, good and true and pure. Amen.

IN THE LATE WINTER

(In the late winter toward the early spring, the pastor may bring into the pulpit bare branches which have swollen buds. Holding these in his hands, he may offer the following prayer.)

O GOD, we thank you for the wonderful power of life which you give to all things. We thank you that though the branches of trees have seemed bare this winter, you have kept alive the sap in the tree and in their branches. We thank you for the buds which are now swelling, which have been safely protected from the frost and the icy wind and the cold snow. We thank you that these buds will soon blossom and bloom, showing us how wonderful is your power even in the life of the tiny bud.

O Lord, all your works are very wonderful, and we thank you for them. We thank you that the winter will soon be over and the spring will be here when the time of the singing of birds will come again. We thank you for being the wonderful Creator, and we ask that we may serve you faithfully all our lives. In Jesus' name, we pray. Amen.

IN SPRINGTIME

(In springtime the minister may hold in his hands a large bouquet of daffodils, or if he prefers, a bouquet of tulips. After this prayer he may give the flowers to the boys and girls to carry to their departments to be placed in a vase on the table as part of the worship center, or he may give a flower to each child.)

OUR FATHER, GOD, how lovely of you to give us these beautiful daffodils (tulips). We thank you that while the bulbs were sleeping under the frozen ground, you did not forget to wake them up and to send the sun to warm the blanket of earth spread over them. We are glad for these brave flowers which are not afraid of March and April winds. They do not fight the wind but nod and dance with the waving winds in happy company. Help us boys and girls, like the daffodils (tulips), to be bright and beautiful, giving joy to our parents and friends always. For Jesus' sake, we pray. Amen.

illustrations

(Illustrations directed to children in the adult sermon)

FORGIVENESS

JOHN WAS getting better as he lay in his bed in the hospital. In the bed next to him was another boy named Bill. They had been in the same room for several weeks, and after a time they began to quarrel. Bill said mean things to John, and John said mean things to Bill.

That night, when the nurse was fixing John up for the night and tucking him into bed, he was so angry he said to her, "That old Bill is a meanie. I'll never forgive him as long as I live."

The nurse said, "Now, John, it is not right to feel that way. Supposing you should die in the night, then you would be sorry that you had never forgiven Bill."

John thought seriously for a few minutes, and then he said, "Well, all right, if I die in the night, I will forgive him, but if I don't die, in the morning Bill better watch out."

Forgiveness must be very deep and real, and not just something we will do if we die.

EXCUSES FOR QUARRELS

ONE DAY I heard about two boys who had been in a fight. When a grown man came along he said, "See here, boys, what are you fighting for and what is the dispute all about?" There had been the sound of crying and the noise of a slap on the boy's face.

Finally one of the boys said, trying to excuse himself, "Well, I knew that he was going to hit me, so I hit him back first."

Isn't it strange the excuses we can make when we want to hit somebody? "He was going to hit me, so I hit him back first." I would call that borrowing a fight.

A NEW SKIPPER

DR. F. B. MYER, famous London preacher, once told about an old

tug which ran between London and Portsmouth, England. It was a queer-shaped, ugly old craft. All the men and sailors along the shore and the docks called this tug, "Old-bust-'em-up."

The reason the old tug was given this name was because she was always bumping into other boats. Whenever she came into dock to tie up, she would always thump and damage some other boat, or run into the dock, or damage the dock gates. She was very clumsily managed by her skipper.

Then, one day, everybody looked in wonder and amazement, for there was Old-bust-'em-up coming into the dock straight as an arrow flies, keeping clear of all other vessels, not bumping any other boat, and not hitting the dock. She slid like a swan into her place securely in the dock.

An old sailor who stood on the wharf could not hold his peace when he saw Old-bust-'em-up coming in safely and decently. He put his hands to his mouth and shouted out toward the tug, "What ho, Old-bust-'em-up, what's happened to you now?"

One of the sailors standing prow of the tug shouted back, "We've got the same old boat, governor, but we've got a new skipper on board."

You see, it does make a difference who is the captain of a ship; whether or not he has the skill and experience to handle the ship. Some people have called Jesus "our Pilot," because he knows how to help us sail a straight, true course in life and reach the harbor of our destination safely.

THE INVENTOR OF THE TELEPHONE

WHEN YOU PICK up the telephone to talk with your friends, don't forget that they called the inventor, Alexander Graham Bell, "Crazy Bell." Well, who was "Crazy Bell"? Crazy Bell was born in Edinburgh, Scotland, the third of three brothers. His two brothers died of tuberculosis.

Young Alexander fell ill, too. The doctors gave him only six months to live. So his father, Professor Bell, took his son to Canada to the town of Brantford in Ontario, where he was to recover his health in the strong, pure air.

When he was twenty-three years of age, Alexander went to live in Boston where he became acquainted with the philosopher, Ralph Waldo Emerson, and the poets, Oliver Wendell Holmes and Henry Wadsworth Longfellow.

Here Alexander became interested in trying to help those who were deaf to be able to speak and to read lips. One of his students was a beautiful girl by the name of Mabel who had never been able to hear anything since she was a baby. While young Alexander Graham Bell was teaching his deaf student, he fell in love with her.

Meanwhile, he turned his talents to invention, and out of his interest in voice and in sound hoped to develop, through means of wires and electricity, the power to transmit the human voice over wires. To many people the idea was so utterly ridiculous that they called him "Crazy Bell." Mabel's father and mother served notice on Alexander that he could not marry their daughter unless he stopped wasting his time trying to make inventions, or could perfect his invention before too long.

One night, Alexander Graham Bell's keen ears heard the faint sounds of a human voice coming over the wires and mouthpiece he had invented. Soon friends became interested and provided the money for the building of the first telephone. Many people still made fun of it, and Western Union rejected it as just an "electrical toy."

At last Mabel's parents consented to their marriage and Alexander Graham Bell had the double joy of winning the girl he loved and seeing his invention of the telephone a success.

Alexander Graham Bell never forgot that if he had not been keenly interested in trying to help other people, and trying to show deaf people how to read lips and how to talk, which compelled him to study the human voice and the transmission of speech, he might never have invented this wonderful, modern instrument we call the telephone. His kindness to deaf-mutes had started him on the road to one of the most marvelous inventions of our day.

THE PICCOLO PLAYER

WHEN SIDNEY LANIER, the great southern poet, was a student at Johns Hopkins University, he played the piccolo in the Baltimore Symphony Orchestra.

One day they were having rehearsal for a concert, and all about young Sidney were violins and trumpets and horns and drums and cymbals going full blast, making a tremendous musical volume.

Suddenly a queer idea came to the young piccolo player. He thought, "If I stopped playing my tiny little instrument, it would never be missed amid all this noise. Why don't I just give up and rest? My little piccolo notes will never be missed."

So he stopped playing, even though he still held the piccolo to his lips as if he were playing.

Instantly, the conductor of the Baltimore Symphony Orchestra rapped loudly with his baton and called every instrument to an immediate stop. With an angry frown he demanded, "Where is the piccolo?" and pointed his baton at Sidney Lanier, who almost jumped out of his seat, he was so frightened.

Not till then had Sidney Lanier realized that even his little notes were so important to the conductor. Then for the first time he understood that the little notes of the piccolo were all a part of the great symphony and very necessary to the harmony, and that the keen and sensitive ear of the conductor would immediately miss them, if he did not play his part.

From that day forward as a student, as a soldier, and as a poet, Sidney Lanier always played his part, even if it were only the small part of a piccolo player.

HOW THE RED CROSS WAS FOUNDED

CLARA BARTON, called "the angel of the battlefield," was born on Christmas Day over one hundred years ago in a little farmhouse in North Oxford, Massachusetts.

When she was only eleven years old, her brother fell from the peak of the barn and for two years he lay in his bed not able to get up, even to take a few steps. Though she was so young, Clara devoted herself as a nurse to her brother, never leaving his bedside for two whole years except for one half-day. She almost forgot that there was any world outside her own house. Her own health was weakened, but she had learned what her lifework was to be—nursing men who were broken and injured.

Though she was only five feet and three inches tall when she was a grown woman and always seemed frail, Clara Barton had a tremendous energy when there was any need for her help.

When she was working in Washington as a stenographer, the War between the States broke out, and Clara Barton immediately began collecting money and clothing for the wounded soldiers. When she heard about the sufferings of the wounded and dying soldiers, she demanded to go to the battlefield to nurse them personally. But at that time there was no Red Cross in the United States, and it was considered a disgrace for a woman to be seen with soldiers near a battlefield.

169

At long last, however, she persuaded the officers of the Army to let her come with her bandages and medicines and her healing touch to minister to the wounded soldiers. The soldiers cheered her up and down the line whenever they knew she was coming. She was an angel of mercy to them.

Illustrations

After the War between the States was ended, war broke out between France and Prussia. The daughter of the King of Prussia asked Clara Barton to come to Europe to direct the relief work of the Red Cross. She was still in poor health, but on the battlefields and in the captured cities of ruin and devastation in Europe, she nursed and clothed and comforted the war-stricken sufferers.

When she returned to the United States, Clara Barton worked hard to persuade our President and senators to establish the International Red Cross in the United States. After ten years of strenuous effort with some friends and associates, she finally had the joy of seeing President Arthur on the first of March, 1882, sign the papers making the United States a member of the International Red Cross. Clara Barton was herself the first national president of the Red Cross. Even at ninety years of age, she traveled west to carry out her Red Cross duties. One of the greatest things she ever said was, "All through and through, thought and act, body and soul, I hate war."

Whenever we hear of the Red Cross coming to the relief of people when there are floods, cyclones, epidemics, forest fires, hurricanes or wars, let us remember that it was this frail woman whose energy and example gave us the Red Cross, here in the United States, and who made possible the service of relief which is now given in every emergency and disaster through that great organization.

GOD IS AT YOUR WINDOW

FOR OVER two years, thirty depressing months, the wife of Fridtjof Nansen, the great explorer of the Arctic, sat beside her lonely window in Oslo, Norway, endlessly waiting for news from her husband that never came. He had gone north with his ship, but the long-unheard-of party of Arctic explorers was thought to be all dead.

No word came back to Oslo from the silence of the great frozen north. The explorer's wife, Mrs. Nansen, knew that her husband was brave, but she was driven to despair knowing how cruel the frozen Arctic is. So every morning she went to her window to look out to see if news were coming.

170   One day there came a little panting, fainting pigeon fluttering down

out of the sky. It landed on the window sill. Mrs. Nansen flung the window open. She grasped the shivering pigeon to her breast, holding it close in her trembling hand, kissed its cold feathers, and hugged it again and again. She knew the long, weary miles that the messenger pigeon had flown. After it had been released from the ship, she knew how it had battled its way across the waste of ice and snow, nursing in its tired, little breast a sense of direction for its home destination.

She looked closely at the legs of the pigeon. To its leg was tied a tiny quill. She opened the quill and inside was a bit of tissue paper. On it were written only three words, "All is well."

There are many windows that we can open toward the sky. By birds and flowers, by friends and church, by the holy Bible, and by Christ himself, God sends his message to us. This is his beautiful message that comes to us from another world, "For God so loved the world that he gave his only Son, that whoever believes in him should not perish but have eternal life."

THE STORY OF JANE ADDAMS

AN AMERICAN college girl, who was touring London, looked down from the top of a bus upon the poor people on the streets of the London slums. They were underfed and thin and sick looking. Rotten cabbages, sold for a penny, were being nervously eaten, unwashed and raw, by the half-starved poor of London.

Jane Addams could not get over what she had seen, and her great heart was moved in pity. She decided that she would go back and become a missionary for the poor of some American city. She would dedicate her life to the service of God.

She went to Chicago and there bought an old mansion in the very heart of one of Chicago's neediest and poorest sections. This was the beginning of her famous settlement house to help and educate the poor, the house called Hull House.

Here for fifty years Jane Addams gave herself to the poor of Chicago who lived among its crowded tenements. With the love of God in her own heart, she made her life a gospel of love and kindness in the shabby tenement district of a great American city. She stood for peace and good will, against all injustice of every shape and kind.

Jane Addams was a very devout Christian and attended the prayer meeting in the Methodist church. She never forgot these verses which

171

she had underlined in her New Testament: "And Jesus went about all the cities and villages . . . healing every sickness and every disease among the people. But when he saw the multitudes, he was moved with compassion on them."

NARCISSUS

ONE OF THE stories that the Greeks liked to tell was the story of Narcissus, son of a river god and of a nymph, distinguished above all others for his beautiful form and face. It was prophesied of Narcissus that he would have a long, long life, if he never looked upon his own features. But this was too much of a temptation for him, because he loved himself so much.

One day Narcissus stood a long time and looked at the image of himself in the mirror made by the water. Immediately, he fell in love with his own reflection. So he missed the length and fullness of life, because he had a narrow focused attention upon himself as the Number One person of importance.

Now, whenever we hear of people who fall in love with themselves, who become narrow and selfish, we think of the myth of Narcissus and feel sorry for them, because we know they are missing the full joy of life.

EVERYONE MAKES MISTAKES

IN THE FAMOUS Rose Bowl football game of 1929 at Pasadena, California, the two teams pitted against each other were Georgia Tech and Southern California. The captain of the Southern California football team was a young man named Ray Riegles. In the course of that game he made a long distance run down the gridiron for a touchdown. He made the only score that was made in the game by this furious dash. But he did not score for his own team, because he had run in the wrong direction. You see, in the excitement of the game he had become confused as to which was his own goal. By running in the wrong direction, he actually had made a touchdown for the opposing Georgia Tech team, and helped them to win. Deep down inside himself, Ray Riegles knew he had let his team down by making this awful mistake.

In the time between the two halves of the game, when the players walk off the field, they always go into the field house where the coach talks to them. Sometimes he talks to them about their mistakes and sometimes about the plays he wants them to use in the second half of the game.

172

All the people who were watching the football game in the stadium that day could not help but wonder what Coach Price was saying to Captain Riegles about the terrible mistake he had made. They did not know until afterward that the coach had never even mentioned Riegles' wrong-direction run. Those who had watched the game were at first surprised and then tremendously delighted when they saw the team walking out on the field again. They noticed that the coach had his arm around the shoulders of Captain Riegles. Then they saw the coach give him a pat of encouragement as he went back into the game to play his part the best he knew how.

DONNY

DONNY WAS a boy whom Mr. and Mrs. Doss had adopted as their own, because he had been left all alone in the world and nobody wanted him. When Donny came into this new family with his adopted parents, Mr. and Mrs. Doss, they all loved him even though he had so much curiosity and energy, and was getting into so many messes that they had to nickname him "Dennis the Menace."

He now belonged to a famous family that lived in a minister's house. He belonged to the "Family Nobody Wanted." You see, the father and mother hunted up orphans whom nobody else would adopt because somehow nobody seemed to want them. Into this wonderful family, Mr. and Mrs. Doss brought baby girls and baby boys, and they loved them all, whether their skins were white, or brown, or yellow, or red, or mixed colors.

Donny loved all the adopted babies, too, but still he kept saying, "I want a brother the size of me." He did not want just babies. He knew that sometimes Mr. and Mrs. Doss went to the place where there were orphan babies waiting for adoption and brought them home to live with Donny, but because they always brought home babies, Donny said they were always getting children "the wrong sizes."

When a year had gone by, and no brother "the size of me" came to Donny, he wrote a letter to Santa Claus. Still nothing happened.

The next year Donny wrote the letter to the lady who owned the orphanage, though he did not know her name. He wrote, "Dear Lady, I want a brother nine years old. (Only Donny could not spell very well, so he wrote "bother" for "brother"). I got lots of room for a new bother the size of me."

One day a letter came from the orphanage lady saying to Mr. and Mrs. Doss, "Now we have a boy just the size of Donny. He is Chip-

173

pewa Indian and Canadian on one side and Blackfoot Indian and Scottish-American on the other side." Then she said, "But he has had so little love that he is shy, sullen, and not friendly."

Illustrations

When Donny heard the news, he could hardly wait for the train to come bringing his new brother, half Chippewa Indian and half Blackfoot Indian. Donny danced up and down on the platform awaiting for the train to come in. At last he saw his new brother getting off the train.

Donny rushed up to meet him and said, "I got two beds in my room, which one do you want to sleep in? I got two dogs, which dog do you want? I got two carts, which cart do you want for your very own?"

So on Christmas Day, Donny came home because at last he had a brother "the size of me," and now I ask you, wasn't that a nice Christmas present for Donny?

A CARDBOARD HOUSE

LOUIS E. HALSEY of New York said that next door to his church there were three young boys who played in the yard each day after school. Like all boys, they wanted to build a playhouse. They took large cartons and spent many wonderful hours building a playhouse. So long as the sun was shining, they had wonderful fun.

Then one day the first storm of winter came. There was rain pelting down, then sleet, and snow, and wind. The cardboard became damp and wet. The rain weakened the boxes and the sleet pelted them. Very soon the winds came and blew the pieces of their playhouse all over the neighborhood.

As the boys looked upon the ruins of their house which had blown away, they said, "Well, we know now for sure that a cardboard house does not stand."

"Yes," said one of the boys, "I remember our Sunday school lesson last Sunday. Jesus told about a man who built his house upon the sand, and the rain descended and the floods came, and it was swept away. Well, I guess a cardboard house is something like that. You have to put good stuff into a house, if you want it to stand, and besides all that, you have to give it a good foundation."

RACE RELATIONS

ONE DAY Jim's mother said, "For twenty-five cents, you can send away for a package of mixed flower seeds. Many varieties of flowers will grow from this package of seeds. I think you would have fun seeing how many different flowers can come from one tiny package."

Jim thought that was a good idea, so he sat down and wrote a letter to the seed company, and enclosed a quarter.

When the small envelope of seeds came, he planted them all in his garden. Then he waited for the sunshine and the rain and the springtime to help them grow.

Each day Jim would go out and see some little green shoots coming up. Some had leaves of one shape, some had leaves of another shape. Some grew tall, some were short. And then the flowers began to appear. Some of the flowers were white, others were brilliant red, but other flowers were dark brown and bronze and deep red, and some were pale yellow.

"Mother, come out here and see how many different flowers I have," Jim would say.

Then his mother replied, "Jim, do you love all the flowers? Do you like the dark brown ones as well as the white ones? Do you like the red ones as well as the yellow ones?"

Jim would always say, "Oh, yes, I think they are all pretty."

Then Jim's mother said, "Well, I am glad you like all the different colors, for God has put many people in his world who are of different colors, too. Each race and each nation has its own attractiveness, its own special form and beauty. Just as your garden is prettier because you have a variety of flowers, so the world is richer for its variety of people."

DR. ALBERT SCHWEITZER

DR. ALBERT SCHWEITZER, the famous missionary doctor and musician, who ministers to the black man below the equator in Africa, grew up as a lad in the town of Gunsbach in Alsace-Lorraine. Because his father was a minister, the young boy Albert was better off than the village boys with whom he went to school. They wore wooden clogs instead of leather shoes. They had no overcoats, and their caps were old brown caps that pulled down over the ears.

One day on his way home from school, young Albert Schweitzer got into a fight with George Nitschelm, who was bigger than he and who was supposed to be stronger. Nevertheless, with a bit of hard fisting and the right twists, Albert got George down and sat on top of him.

While the bigger boy was lying under Schweitzer, the boy jerked out and stood up and said to Schweitzer, through the tears he was striving hard to hold back, "Yes, you got me down, but if I had broth to eat twice a week as you do, I should be as strong as you are."

That sentence stabbed the tender heart of young Albert Schweitzer. He realized that though the older boy was bigger, he himself was stronger because he had better food to eat and came from a home where he had better things. George had spoken with cruel plainness, and young Schweitzer went home with a guilty feeling.

Ever after that, Albert Schweitzer had compassion on the other poor boys of the village and did not want to be different from them. He refused to wear the new overcoat his parents bought him, because the other boys had none. He refused to wear leather shoes on week-days, because the other boys had to wear wooden clogs. He refused to put on a handsome, new sailor's cap his mother bought him, because the other boys did not have good caps.

From that moment onward, Albert Schweitzer was always kind to animals and kind to the poor, until at last one day God called him to be a missionary doctor to the poorest of the poor, the black men in Africa.

Because he has been so kind in Jesus' name to these poor black men, the world honors Dr. Albert Schweitzer today as one of the wisest, happiest, and most noble men who has ever lived.

IN YOUR OWN BACK YARD

MOST BOYS and girls have sometimes sold tickets to their own amateur side shows or kodachrome slide lectures or movie shows. Sometimes, however, it is best to beware of buying your ticket, unless you think seriously about what you are going to see.

Rufus M. Jones tells about Charles Carrol Everett, a Harvard University professor, who, when he was a little boy, heard that there was going to be an eclipse of the sun. His father told him that he would be able to see the eclipse from his own back yard. The young boy, Charles Carrol Everett, took advantage of this opportunity and had little tickets made which he sold to all his boy friends, telling them that they could see the eclipse of the sun from his back yard. A ten-cent ticket would admit each boy to his back yard.

The boys paid the dimes. They all came into his back yard and looked at the eclipse of the sun. Very soon, however, they discovered that they could have seen the eclipse just as well in their own back yards.

But that is the way with people, they like to go over the fence into some other yard, or over into another pasture where they think the grass is greener. They forget what wonderful things can be seen, even from their own back yards.

KINDNESS TO ANIMALS

FROM HIS EARLIEST years Albert Schweitzer, the famous medical missionary and great musician, has always felt pity for the poor and compassion for the sick. He once said that as long as he can remember he was always saddened by the amount of misery he saw in the world.

Even as a boy he was kind to animals, for he could not bear to see them suffer pain. For weeks at a time he could not forget the sight of a poor, old, lame horse limping along and being beaten with a stick by the driver.

When he said his prayers at night as a boy, he always prayed that the animals might sleep in peace and be guarded from pain and harm. He always said this prayer silently to himself after his mother had left the room, for he did not think even his mother would understand why he should pray for animals.

When he was only seven years old, some boys who had made rubber slingshots said to him, "Come along, Albert, let's go out and shoot some birds."

Because he was so young, Albert did not have the courage to refuse to go, for fear the other boys would laugh at him; but he was trembling at the thought of shooting any birds.

One of the boys put a stone in his slingshot, aiming it at one of the birds that was singing beautifully with the other birds on the branches of the tree. "With terrible cringes of conscience" young seven-year-old Albert also put a stone into his slingshot, getting ready to shoot.

But just then something wonderful happened. The first warning bell of the village church began to ring loudly. It sounded like a warning voice from heaven. With that, Albert shooed the birds away so that they were safe from the slingshot of his companion.

From that time onward, whenever he heard the church bells ring, Albert always remembered with gratitude how the music of the bells had driven deep into his soul the Commandment, "Thou shalt not kill."

Albert Schweitzer has always been tenderhearted toward all living forms of life, whether man or animal. In his little home in Africa, in his hospital near the equator, where he helps to heal so many sick people, he keeps many tame animals about him, a deer, a dog, a cat, and he loves even the hens and the chickens. Albert Schweitzer has what is called a great feeling of reverence for life, and it all started in his childhood when he was kind to the birds and wanted to protect them.

LOVE

SUSAN WAS only six years old, and she walked into the living room where her daddy was reading the evening paper. On the table beside him was a large globe showing the various countries of the world.

Susan said to her father, "Daddy, where is America on the globe?"

The father turned the globe around until he found America, and putting his finger on the spot he said, "This, my dear, is America." Then he said, "Susan, why did you want me to show you where America is on the globe of the world?"

She answered, "Because, Daddy, I want to kiss it. I love America." And then she put her arms all around the world, as she stood on tiptoe, and kissed America.

So it is if we love God, we not only love our own country, but we put God's arms of love all around the world, and we learn to love all the people of the world for his sake.

WITNESSING FOR CHRIST

A FAMOUS LONDON preacher, Dr. Leslie D. Weatherhead, relates a scene which once took place in Queen's Hall in London. A cultured audience has come to listen to a great concert. One of the numbers on the program is sung by a young girl whose name is unknown. She is greeted by a deafening applause, so she sings the same song again. The audience is not yet satisfied, and demands that she sing it once more. This time as she goes to the platform a great silence sweeps over the audience.

> There is a green hill far away
>> Without a city wall,
> Where the dear Lord was crucified,
>> Who died to save us all.

The effect is tremendous. It is electrical. Not for a long time have these jaded city concertgoers listened to any religious message and some of them not for years have heard a word of hope from the Cross.

Her beautiful voice goes on:

> Oh, dearly, dearly has He loved,
>   And we must love Him, too.
> And trust in His redeeming blood,
>   And try His works to do.

There are no dry eyes in the audience. The soloist doesn't bow this time. There is no applause, only a great silence.

—Adapted from *The Secret Place.*